More praise for *Bodies in Motion and at Rest*

"Eloquent . . . unabashed lyricism. . . . [Lynch] has a capacious understanding of human foibles and a great tolerance for them. . . . It is impossible not to take him seriously, since he is deeply thoughtful and his
thoughts have been hammered out on the anvil of experience. It is also
impossible not to like him, because his voice is rich and generous."
—Richard Bernstein, *New York Times*

"The eloquence of these studies, the ingenuity of these meditations, and
the wit of these terminations (surely the right word here) afford Lynch his
continuity with Sir Thomas Browne and with Donne's *Biathanatos*: his
plot, as is said in the trade, is neat, and his mortality *remains*."
—Richard Howard

"[A] thought-provoking, engaging hybrid of memoir, meditation, and
comic monologue. . . . Lynch approaches his subjects with a beautifully
executed balance of irreverence with reverence, gallows humor with
emotional delicacy, and no-nonsense immanence with lyrical transcen-
dence." —*New York Times Book Review*

"It would be almost worth dying to have [Lynch] at your funeral, not only
because of his humor (like Garrison Keillor's, but richer) but mainly because
he is . . . the embodiment of an antidote to our increasingly impersonal
world. Lynch has his finger on the bloody pulse of creation, and what
makes him such a fine essayist is that's it's just the business of everyday
life and death to him. Death is so much a part of creation that it's hardly
even an ending, and Lynch writes most beautifully in these essays about
passage and about echoes throughout generations."
—*Los Angeles Times Book Review*, A Best Book of 2000

"Lynch . . . brings the incantatory beauty of poetry to his wryly philosoph-
ical and finely crafted prose in his superb second essay collection. . . . As
Lynch ponders love, loss, and the routines of existence, the unabashedly
emotional voice of his Irish ancestors lies with his Midwestern matter-of-
factness to create a bracing blend of empathy and humor, stoicism and
deep feeling." —Donna Seaman, *Booklist*

"The grace note of Lynch's work is that his awareness of death has sharpened his sense of humor. . . . Lynch has a true poetic gift for odd digressionary commentary connections that feel right."

—*New Orleans Times-Picayune*

"Lynch's writing is like his preferred subject: It takes your breath away."

—*Chicago New City*

"This is poetic prose in the best sense, full of intricate internal correspondences, and ordered by a magical discipline that allows the reader to feel most keenly what is most carefully hidden." —*Houston Chronicle*

"[Lynch] thinks with the associative freedom of a poet, leaping with intuitive accuracy from the personal to the public and back again, mingling idea and anecdote, wandering widely." —*San Francisco Chronicle*

"[*Bodies in Motion and at Rest*] . . . bears an incorruptible load of joy, tears, wit and revelation . . . worthy of [Lynch's] ancestral ties to the Seamus Heaneys and W. B. Yeatses he so reveres."

—*Indianapolis Star*

"Mr. Lynch writes with such clarity and imagination and grace, I stopped on nearly every page to savor an image, a connection or a paragraph of staggering originality and wit."

—Tom Mayo, *Dallas Morning News*

"[Lynch] continues his exploration of the human condition with humor and insight and his constant search for what Hemingway called 'the one true word.'" —citation for Great Lakes Book Award

▲ *Bodies in Motion*
AND AT REST ▼

BY THOMAS LYNCH

Poems

Skating with Heather Grace
Grimalkin & Other Poems
Still Life in Milford

Essays

The Undertaking—Life Studies from the Dismal Trade

▲ *Bodies in Motion*
AND AT REST ▼

essays by
Thomas Lynch

W. W. Norton & Company
New York / London

Since this page cannot legibly accommodate all the copyright notices, pages
17–18 constitute an extension of the copyright page.

For information about permission to reproduce selections from this book,
write to Permissions, W. W. Norton & Company, Inc.,
500 Fifth Avenue, New York, NY 10110

The text of this book is composed in New Caledonia
with the display set in New Caledonia and Trajan.
Composition by Sue Carlson
Manufacturing by Haddon Craftsmen
Book design by BTDnyc

Library of Congress Cataloging-in-Publication Data

Lynch, Thomas, 1948–
Bodies in motion and at rest : on metaphor and mortality / Thomas Lynch.
p.   cm.
ISBN 0-393-04927-2
ISBN 0-393-32164-9 pbk.
1. Life. I. Title.
BD431.L97   2000
113'.8—dc21   00-021355

W. W. Norton & Company, Inc., 500 Fifth Avenue, New York, N.Y. 10110
www.wwnorton.com

W. W. Norton & Company Ltd.
Castle House, 75/76 Wells Street, London W1T 3QT
1 2 3 4 5 6 7 8 9 0

This book is for

Tom, Heather, Michael and Sean,

and for

Mary Tata.

Gentlemen, songsters, off on a spree
Doomed from here to eternity.
Lord, have mercy on such as we,
Baa! Baa! Baa!
—from "The Whiffenpoof Song" by MEADE MINNEGERODE,
as derived from RUDYARD KIPLING

Sometimes I need love's answer to the question
about the breathing creatures and their pain.
I shouldn't be comfortable with the easy one
that claims the very daylight is a sign
of transubstantial warmth among the stars—
though there was brightness over town and countryside.
—from "A Sign from Heaven" in *Love's Answer*
by MICHAEL HEFFERNAN

E pur si muove!
(And yet it moves!)
—GALILEO GALILEI, after his recantation

Contents

Acknowledgments

Books do not come into being on their own. The essays assembled here, while written in private, owe their being to a wider community of colleagues, neighbors, friends and family. In all these I have been richly blessed.

Apart from the editors of journals and newspapers who commissioned and published these pieces, I am also grateful to the many organizations that have invited me to speak from their particular lecterns. Such forums have been both proving grounds and field studies for my work. In addition to the colleges, universities and state and national funeral service associations that have made me feel welcome, I am grateful to Dean Alastair G. Hunter of the School of Divinity at the University of Glasgow, to the Last Acts Campaign and the Robert Wood Johnson Foundation, to the New Jersey Hospice and Palliative Care Association, to the New York Citizens Committee on Health Care Decisions, to the Arvon Foundation, to the National Book Foundation, to the Before Columbus Foundation and to the Chautauqua Institution.

If not for the dedication of colleagues and staff at Lynch & Sons Funeral Directors, I would not be free to pursue these interests. To Edward Lynch, Wesley and Betty Rice, Ken Kutzli, Karen Kramb, Becca Ward, Norm Garnett, Matthew Sheffler, Ruth Gibson, Thelma Connely, Jack and Virginia Baker, George Woodworth, Timothy Lynch, Michael and Mary Howell, Julie Kenrick, Brigid Lynch, Michael Lynch, and Sean Lynch I am deeply appreciative, as I am to the communities we serve for the trust they continue to place in us.

To have friends who are poets is no bad thing. To Matthew Sweeney, A. L. Kennedy, Keith Taylor, Richard Tillinghast, Philip Casey, Dennis O'Driscoll and Louise Guinness I am indebted for their valuable commentaries on this work, as I am to David Eason, the Reverend John Harris and the Reverend Jacob Andrews.

I am most especially indebted to the poet Michael Heffernan, whose friendship is dear to me and without whose tutelage I might never have taken up a writing life.

To have poets for editors is a gift. For Robin Robertson of Jonathan Cape in London and Jill Bialosky of W. W. Norton in New York I give daily thanks, as I do for Richard P. McDonough, my loyal agent and advocate.

Wilson Beebe, John Eirkson, the late Howard Raether and the Reverend Thomas Long have been generous with their insights into the place of the funeral in our culture and marketplace, as have Joseph Dumas, Lisa Carlson, Constancia Romilly and Benjamin Treuhaft.

In matters mortuary and familial, my chief consultant is my brother Patrick Lynch—a great man entirely and the finest funeral director I know. In addition to his wisdoms, it is my good fortune to have those of Colonel Daniel Lynch and Christopher Lynch, the oldest and youngest of my brothers, respectively.

I am deeply indebted to the family and friends who have allowed me to write about their lives. Where necessary, in particular with regards to the local dead and their families, I have changed names or made composites of characters in an effort to protect their privacy.

The following dedications of individual essays are made with thanks: "Bodies in Motion and at Rest" to the memory of Ronald Willis; "Bible Studies" to Larry Keef and the men we meet with on Tuesday mornings at the Big Boy; "The Way We Are" to Marty P. and the friends we meet with on Sunday mornings at Maplegrove; "Funerals-R-Us" to the memory of Howard Raether; and "The Oak Grove Imbroglio" to Mary Jackson.

For my daughter, Heather Grace, and my sons Tom, Mike and Sean I give thanks to God; and to them I give thanks for all they have taught me about life.

The account I keep with Mary Tata is a gift like grace—abundant, undeserved, permanent.

Credits

To the editors of *Esquire, Harper's, Newsweek, The Daily Telegraph Magazine, The New York Times Magazine, The Independent, The Washington Post, The Boston Globe, The Irish Times, The New York Times, The Times* of London, the *San Francisco Chronicle, The Washington Post, The Paris Review, Poetry East,* Fodor's guides, the *American Funeral Director, The Southern Review, The Cresset,* and *Witness,* where the essays collected here, or portions of them, first appeared, the author is grateful.

"Wombs" first appeared in *Body,* an anthology edited by Sharon Sloan Fiffer and Steve Fiffer, published by Bard in 1999.

Several of these essays were recorded in West Clare and Rotterdam for broadcast on BBC Radio 4 by Kate McAll, producer, to whom the author also wishes to make known his thanks.

For permission to reprint copyright material, the author and the publishers gratefully acknowledge the following:

Extracts from "October Salmon" by Ted Hughes, from *New*

Introduction

People sometimes ask me why I write. Because, I tell them, I don't golf. This gives me two or three days a week—five or six the way my brother was doing it before he had a midlife crisis and took up rollerblades. But a couple of days every week at least, with a few hours in them in which to read or write. It's all the same thing to me, reading and writing, twins of the one conversation. We're either speaking or are spoken to. And I don't drink. I did, of course, and plenty of it, but had to quit for the usual reasons. It got to where I was spilling so much of it. This gave me two or three nights a week—five or six the way I was doing it at the end—with a few hours in them when things weren't blurry. With some of those hours I would read or write. And I am married to an Italian woman with some French sensibilities and five brothers, so I am home most nights, and when I'm not, I call. I sleep well, rise early, and since I don't do Tae Bo or day trading, I read or write a few hours each morning. Then I take a walk. Out there on Shank's mare, I think about what I'm reading or writing, which is one of the things I really like—it's portable. You don't need a caddy or a designated driver or a bag full of cameras. All you need's a little peace and quiet and the words will come to you—your own or the other's. Your own voice or the voice of God. Perspiration, inspiration. It feels like a gift.

Years ago I was watching a woman undress. The room was lit only by the light of the moon coming through an easterly window. Everything about this moment was careless and beautiful except for the sound of a sick boy in the next room coughing and croupy, unable to sleep. He had his medicine. The VapoRub and steam were bubbling away. I was drowsing with the sounds and darkening images, half dreaming of Venice, the Lido and the Zattere, the tall windows of a room I stayed in once, awash in moonlight and shadows, longing for the woman I loved madly then. It was that sweet moment between wake and sleep when the dream has only a foot in the door that the day and its duties have left ajar. I wanted always to remember that sweetness, that moment, and knew I could not rise to write the details down—the sick child, the woman's beauty, the moonlight, the steam bubbling, the balance between the dream and duty, between the romance and the ordinary times—because the slumber was tightening around me. And I was searching for a word, one word that I could keep and remember till the morning; one word only: a key, a password by which I could return to this moment just long enough to make a poem, a purse made of words to keep the treasure of it in. And I was fading quickly, my eyes were closed, my last bit of consciousness was clinging to words then bits of words and finally only bits of noises, the woman beside me, the boy's labored but even breathing, the bubbling of the *vaporizer*, which became in my dream the *vaporetti* idling in the Grand Canal, because it was the key—*vaporetti*—the password, the outright gift of sound whose bubbling and whose syllables sound near enough the same as the *vaporizer* in the next room to let me traffic back and forth at will between the bedroom in Michigan and the bedroom in Venice and the moonlight and the beauty and the moment awash in ivory and shimmering images. I slept with the word. I woke with it. I rose and wrote the poem down. The women are gone. The boy is grown. The poem sits on the shelf in a book. I come and go to Venice as I please. The language is alive and well.

So this is why I write and read. Because I don't golf, and I don't drink, and I'm married to an Italian, and every day I sit down to it, there's the chance that I might get another *vaporetti,* another gift, another of what Hemingway calls the "one true word" that will make some sense out of what we're doing here. That part about Hemingway I heard on the radio. Keep your ears tuned. Words are everywhere.

Today, for example—it is September, the last late summer of the century. Planes have fallen from the sky. Trains are colliding. There's trouble in the Balkans. Farmers are worried about drought and prices. Earthquakes in Turkey. Hurricanes off the Carolinas. Death tolls are rising. Tax cuts and national debt are in the news. The political soap opera carries on. The day is already full of words. I'm listening.

What, as St. Paul asked famously, are we to say to these things? What is the one true word today? What is the word that becomes flesh? The gospel? The good word, the good news? The truth, the whole truth? The will of God? What's a man of my age and my times to make of it all on any given day if he doesn't golf or drink or gallivant? Is bearing a little witness the best I can do?

This morning I was reading the letters of Paul. The one to the Romans is about circumcision, about faith and works, about sin and the law. No wonder he seems to go in circles a bit.

He's telling the Romans that they don't have to become Jews to become Christians. The earliest Christians were Jews, of course, including, it is worth repeating, Jesus Himself or himself, depending on your particulars. Guilt and shame are ecumenical and have always worked for observant Christians and observant Jews.

Specifically, Paul is telling the Romans that they needn't be circumcised. This is good news on any given day, at least to the men of the congregation. There's a concept they can get behind. Then, as now, women were given to wonder about the things men worry about. The laws about diet and fashions and the keeping of feasts are easy enough and all in line with the rules of good living. But circumcision is a deal breaker and Paul knows it. So he's trying to tell them it's not all that important after all. He's floating this option of "spiritual circumcision." It's a talking point and the numbers look good. Then, too, he doesn't want to offend the brethren back in the Promised Land, who are, it is well known, his kinsmen and the Chosen People. If he devalues the old deal made between God and Abraham, the Old Testament, that early covenant of blood, he's going to lose the very ones who have bought into his take on the Nazarene—the part about Him being the Son of God. Try telling some coreligionist who just had his foreskin removed that it really wasn't necessary and see what happens. This is where the faith and works come in, the part that is so important to Luther fifteen centuries later when the Reformation begins. By deconstructing that section of Genesis where God and Abraham cut their deal, Paul is able to coax both Gentile and Jew in the direction of his version of things. Here is a man who is able to make both those with foreskins and those without feel good about themselves. It's a bit like watching a game of Twister, but it is a deft little exercise in the use of language.

Language, some right thinker said, is a dialect with a navy. Much the same can be said for religions—whatever the word is, they need a navy or an army to spread it. Paul is Christianity's navy. He has some impressive character flaws—he's pompous, opinionated, opportunistic, misogynistic, vexed by sexuality in general and, like any true believer, a dangerous man. Before he came to his senses he was slaughtering Christians with enthusiasm. Still, no one can say he's not willing to travel, to "take it to them" in our latter-day parlance, to walk the walk that goes with the talk. No doubt he'll remind you of someone you know. Maybe your husband or father or brother-in-law. Today he'd be a radio talk-show host or TV preacher, prime minister or lately retired Speaker of the House. Women would be uniformly offended by and attracted to him, each for reasons unique to themselves, none of which would have to do with circumcision. All the same it should be said that Time, such as we know it, would be nothing without the travels of Paul and his letters. We would not all be hovering over the changing of millennia, fretting about disasters and apocalypse and computer glitches. We would not have divided Time into B.C. and A.D., because whether C(hrist) was D(omine) was pretty much up for grabs until Paul got knocked off his horse and saw the light. But for that today would be just another day in the year of some pagan deity.

So today neither dialects nor religions need navies or armies or missionaries as much as they need Web sites and wideband space and a lobbyist. Maybe Paul looks a little obsolete, with his horse and epistles and his true belief. And if the business of foreskins isn't what it once was, still, the deals that are cut between blood and belief, tribe and creed, dialect and sect, color and kind, define every age before Paul and since. Then, as now, the haves and the have-nots are badly divided.

So maybe the word today isn't *circumcision*.

Maybe it's *faith* or *works*. Or *sin* and *the law*. Those chicken-and-egg games that Paul rolls out for us to kick around the yard for the rest of history. Did God give Abraham a son in old age and make him the father of nations because of his faith or because of what he was willing to do to prove his faith? If there were no law, would there be no sin? Can ignorance be bliss if not a defense? Your man argues all sides of these and related issues in his letters. The true words are in there blinking, but I cannot find them. Not today. Today I'll have to get by on faith.

Maybe it's not the word today at all. Maybe it's a number. The language is full of them. You could start counting now and never finish. Like words, they've got us, well, outnumbered. All you can do is hunt and peck for the good word, the lucky number, the truth of the matter.

My father's lucky number was thirteen. He was born on the thirteenth and wore number thirteen on his jersey in high school and signed his best deals on the thirteenth of the month and died in a condo that was number thirteen. He always said that thirteen was his number. Who could blame him? So I'm looking at the thirteenth verse of the thirteenth chapter of Paul's letter to the Romans because my wife is Italian and I'm not drinking this morning and no one's coming to take me golfing and here's what it says there, word for word: "Let us live honorably as in the day, not in reveling and drunkenness, not in debauchery and licentiousness, not in quarreling and jealousy." Now, that mightn't make the hairs stand on the back of your neck, but the Romans were done no harm when they heard it and for me it sounds like the voice of my father. Not that he talked like that, mind you, but still it's a concept he could get behind. Because he was the kind of guy who wasn't looking for all the answers. Just enough to get him through the day. Just one little something that rang true enough that he could hang his hat on it when he came home and find it still there in the morning. Unlike Abraham, he didn't want to be the father of a nation. Unlike Paul, he didn't want to save the world. He just wanted his children to outlive him, his wife to love him and everything to work out in the end. It did.

Same for me. Just enough good word to get through the day. It's liable to turn up anywhere—a good book, the Good Book, the bumper of a car, something on the radio, something your daughter says, something that comes to you in a dream, like "Eat more fruit, Adam," or "Say your prayers," which is what my sainted mother frequently says when I dream of her. Or maybe it is something your true love says, like the time mine said, "Everything is going to be all right." I believed her then, I believe her now. Or, let's say you're standing in the shower, counting syllables, when it comes to you that *nine thousand, nine hundred, ninety-nine* has exactly nine syllables in it and is exactly the number of dollars you can deposit in cash without the tax man getting involved, or line those nines up, all four in a row, and they look like the day and the month and the year you're thinking this. Who invented wonders like that? Or maybe it hits you like a bolt of lightning, like *preaching to bishops is like farting at skunks*. What disgruntled cleric first told me that? These are words to live by? I don't know. What if Paul had written them to the Romans? Maybe they'd have learned to lighten up. Maybe they wouldn't have gotten so schismatic after all.

Or maybe you go looking for the one true word, like last fall in Barcelona when I climbed to the top of those towering spires in Gaudí's cathedral, La Sagrada Família. It's a hundred years in the making and not done yet. Maybe they should declare it a shopping mall and finish the thing. Maybe they just like it as a work in progress. Anyway, I'm climbing to the very top of the steeple, overlooking the city like any good pilgrim, and at the top I say "Here I am Lord" and the wind is howling in my ears like Moses on the mountain. "Give me the Good Word, God! I'll cut it in stone." And the city out before me and I'm whispering so that none of the other pilgrims will hear me, but I'm saying it out loud: "Show me a sign and I'll write it down!" And you know what the sign said, the one I first saw when I turned to make my way down from the heights? It said, WATCH YOUR STEP. In Catalan and in English and in Japanese, which is, I suppose, a sign that God speaks in all our tongues. Maybe next time I'll go looking in Venice. Maybe next time I'll take the gondola. Maybe I don't have to go looking at all. Maybe it will come to me. On its own. When I least expect it.

So what are we to make of these things?

You want to get some good words like these? I say don't golf, don't drink, marry an Italian—it could happen to you.

But maybe you'll make a different deal with God. There's other things you want? Instead of words? A scratch game, a good Beaujolais, a date with a shepherd from the Hebrides? That's fine. God knows your heart. God knows you want your children to outlive you, your beloved to love you, everything to work out in the end.

Work hard. Have faith. It will.

One last thing. A word to the wise. Like with me and my father, like with Peter and Paul, like with Moses and Abraham—when dealing with God, or rabbis and bishops, any of that crowd—a thing well worth knowing is where to cut.

—TL

Milford, Michigan

Bodies in Motion
and at Rest

So I'm over at the Hortons'
with my stretcher and mini-
van and my able apprentice,
young Matt Sheffler, because they found old George, the cemetery
sexton, dead in bed this Thursday morning in ordinary time. And
the police have been in to rule out foul play and the EMS team
to run a tape so some ER doctor wired to the world can declare
him dead at a safe distance. And now it's ours to do—Matt's and
mine—to ease George from the bed to the stretcher, negotiate the
sharp turn at the top of the stairs, and go out the front door to the
dead wagon idling in the driveway and back to the funeral home
from whence he'll take his leave—waked and well remembered—
a Saturday service in the middle of April, his death observed, his
taxes due.

We are bodies in motion and at rest—there in George's master bedroom, in the gray light of the midmorning, an hour or so
after his daughter found him because he didn't answer when she

called this morning, and he always answers, and she always calls, so she got in the car and drove over and found him exactly as we find him here: breathless, unfettered, perfectly still, manifestly indifferent to all this hubbub. And he is here, assembled on his bed as if nothing had happened, still propped on his left shoulder, his left ear buried in his pillow, his right leg hitched up over the left one, his right hand tucked up under the far pillow his ex-wife used to sleep on, before she left him twenty years ago, and under the former Mrs. Horton's pillow, I lift to show Matt, is a little pearl-handled .22 caliber that George always slept with since he has slept alone. "Security," he called it. He said it helped him sleep.

And really there is nothing out of order, no sign of panic or struggle or pain, and except for the cardiac-blue tinting around his ears, the faint odor of body heat and a little early rigor in his limbs, which makes the moving of him easier, one'd never guess George wasn't just sleeping in this morning—catching the twenty extra winks—because maybe he'd been up late playing poker with the boys, or maybe he'd had a late dinner with his woman friend, or maybe he was just a little tired from digging graves and filling them, and anyway, he hadn't a grave to open this morning for one of the locals who was really dead.

But this morning George Horton is really dead and he's really being removed from his premises by Matt and me after we swaddle him in his own bed linens, sidle him on to the stretcher, tip the stretcher up to make the tight turn at the top of the stairs and carefully ease it down, trying to keep the wheels from thumping each time the heavier head end of the enterprise takes a step. And it's really a shame, all things considered, because here's George, more or less in his prime, just south of sixty, his kids raised, his house paid off, a girlfriend still in her thirties with whom he maintained twice-weekly relations—"catch as catch can," he liked to say. And he's a scratch golfer and a small business owner with reliable employees and frequent flier miles that he spends on trips to Vegas twice a year, where he lets himself get a little crazy with the crap tables and showgirls. And he has his money tucked into rental homes and mutual funds, and a host of friends who'd only say good things about him, and a daughter about to make him a grandfather for the first time, and really old George seemed to have it made, and except for our moving him feet first down the stairs this morning, he has everything to live for, everything.

And it is there, on the landing of the first floor, only a few feet from the front door out, that his very pregnant daughter waits in her warmup suit to tender her good-byes to the grandfather of her baby, not yet born. And Matt's face is flushed with the lifting, the huffing and puffing, or the weight of it all, or the sad beauty of the woman as she runs her hand along her father's cheek, and she is catching her breath and her eyes are red and wet and she lifts her face to ask me, "Why?"

"His heart, Nancy . . ." is what I tell her. "It looks like he just slept away. He never felt a thing." These are all the well-tested comforts one learns after twenty-five years of doing these things.

"But *why*?" she asks me, and now it is clear that *how* it happened is not good enough. And here I'm thinking all the usual suspects: the cheeseburgers, the whiskey, the Lucky Strikes, the thirty extra pounds we, some of us, carry, the walks we didn't take, the preventive medicines we all ignore, the work and the worry and the tax man, the luck of the draw, the nature of the beast, the way of the world, the shit that happens because it happens.

But Nancy is not asking for particulars. She wants to know why in the much larger, Overwhelming Question sense: why we don't just live forever. Why are we all eventually orphaned and heartbroken? Why we human beings cease to be. Why our nature won't leave well enough alone. Why we are not all immortal. Why this morning? Why George Horton? Why oh why oh why?

No few times in my life as a funeral director have I been asked this. Schoolchildren, the newly widowed, musing clergy, fellow pilgrims—maybe they think it was my idea. Maybe they just like to see me squirm contemplating a world in which folks wouldn't need caskets and hearses and the likes of me always ready and willing and at their service. Or maybe, like me, sometimes they really wonder.

"Do the math" is what George Horton would say. Or "Bottom line." Or "It's par for the course." Or "It's Biblical." If none of these wisdoms seemed to suit, then "Not my day to watch it" is what he'd say. Pressed on the vast adverbials that come to mind whilst opening or closing graves, George could be counted for tidy answers. Self-schooled in the Ways of the World, he confined his reading to the King James Bible, *The Wall Street Journal, Golf Digest*, the *Victoria's Secret* catalog and the Big Book of Alcoholics Anonymous. He watched C-SPAN, The Home Shopping Network and The Weather Channel. Most afternoons he'd doze off watching Oprah, with whom he was, quite helplessly, in love. On quiet days he'd surf the Web or check his portfolio on-line. On Sundays he watched talking heads and went to dinner and the movies with his woman friend. Weekday mornings he had coffee with the guys at the Summit Café before making the rounds of the half dozen cemeteries he was in charge of. Wednesdays and Saturdays he'd mostly golf.

"Do the math" I heard him give out with once from the cab of his backhoe for no apparent reason. He was backfilling a grave in Milford Memorial. "You gonna make babies, you've gotta make some room; it's Biblical."

Or once, leaning on a shovel, waiting for the priest to finish: "Copulation, population, inspiration, expiration. It's all arithmetic—addition, multiplication, subtraction and long division. That's all we're doing here, just the math. Bottom line, we're buried a thousand per acre, or burned into two quarts of ashes, give or take."

There was no telling when such wisdoms would come to him.

BUT IT CAME TO ME, embalming George later that morning, that the comfort in numbers is that they all add up. There is a balm in the known quantities, however finite. Any given year at this end of the millennium, 2.3 million Americans will die. Ten percent of pregnancies will be unintended. There'll be 60 million common colds. These are numbers you can take to the bank. Give or take, 3.9 million babies will be born. It's Biblical. They'll get a little more or a little less of their 76 years of life expectancy. The boys will grow to just over 69 inches, the girls to just under 64. Of them, 25 percent will be cremated, 35 percent will be overweight, 52 percent will drink. Every year 2 million will get divorced, 4 million will get married and there'll be 30,000 suicides. A few will win the lotto, a few will run for public office, a few will be struck by lightning. And any given day, par for the course, 6,300 of our fellow citizens, just like George, will get breathless and outstretched and spoken of in the past tense; and most will be dressed up the way I dress up George, in his good blue suit, and put him in a casket with Matt Sheffler's help, and assemble the 2 or 3 dozen floral tributes and the 100 or 200 family and friends and the 60 or 70 cars that will follow in the 15 mile per hour procession down through town to grave 4 of lot 17 of section C in Milford Memorial, which will become, in the parlance of our trade, his final resting place, over which a 24-by-12-by-4-inch Barre granite stone will be placed, into which we will have sandblasted his name and dates, one of which, subtracted from the other, will amount, more or less, to his life and times. The corruptible, according to the officiating clergy, will have put on incorruption, the mortal will have put on immortality. "Not my day to watch it" will be among the things we'll never hear George Horton say again.

Nor can we see clearly now, looking into his daughter Nancy's eyes, the blue morning at the end of this coming May when she'll stand, upright as any walking wound, holding her newborn at the graveside of the man, her one and only father, for whom her baby will be named. Nor can we hear the promises she makes to keep him alive, to always remember, forever and ever, in her heart of hearts. Nor is there any math or bottom line or Bible verse that adds or subtracts or in any way accounts for the moment or the mystery she holds there.

Sweeney Revisited

No few among my correspondents have made discreet inquiries after the condition of Matthew Sweeney, my dear friend and fellow poet, of Donegal and Dombey Street, London WC 1. The hypochondria he suffers from, about which I've written before at length, is apparently such a widespread condition that it links him with a fair large fraction of his species. If my mail is any sign, his commiserators, if called together for a convention, could fill a small country, an island nation, say, or the state of South Dakota. And it is surely a sign of the Goodness of Man (read Women too) that no sooner had my earlier profile on Mr. Sweeney appeared in a serious British literary venue than I began to receive cards and letters from the similarly afflicted, or the family members and friends of same, from every quarter of the English-speaking world, tendering helpful information on support groups, chat rooms, charitable foundations and what-have-yous that might offer if not outright remedy then some relief from the more disabling symptoms of his condition.

Several daily regimens were among the frequent suggestions: jogging, meditation, oatmeal enemas. The ingestion or injection of neo-coagulants, urine therapy, new recipes of herbal and veggie things; a season at Chautauqua, off-season on Iona. I cataloged them alphabetically. All of these I dutifully passed on to your man, not so much with an expectation that he might take them up but to let him know he is not alone. Grief shared, they say, is grief diminished. The more the merrier. The math of fellow-feeling is precise.

All the same, one symptom of the sickness—quite separate from the sense that no one's ills are as urgent as yours—is the sense, ever there, that nothing whatever will do any good—neither sit-ups nor ginseng tea nor pilgrimages to Medugorje. Nothing will undo the certainty of progressive malady and impending doom. What is worse, as I've said before, any effort to disabuse the hypochondriac of his or her fears is further complicated by a fair body of evidence, which is added to in doses every day in places like Arlington and Highgate and the local obits, that Mr. Sweeney might be on to something—disease and death are, after all, going around.

There is no cure, I'm told, for hypochondria apart, of course, from death itself, which renders all sickness and rude good health, real or imagined, more or less mute. The hypochondriac is therefore a hopeless case, whose illness (the fear of sickness and of death) is most often cured by sickness and death. "I told you so" seems the haunting subtext of their funerals. The suffering ceases only when the sufferer deceases.

One is reminded of Yeats's ever-present genius, to wit: "How can we know the dancer from the dance?"

Still, the outpouring of compassion on Mr. Sweeney's

behalf—the unguents, poultices and folk remedies, the recipes and holy relics, the tinctures and talismans, the Web sites and incantations, the privately bottled potions, medical apparatuses and personal testimonies that came my way, made me begin to think that perhaps there is some hope for Sweeney after all! One woman from a suburb of Cleveland, Ohio, sent me a freeze-dried packet of her ambrosia salad, which could be reconstituted by adding cold water and seasoned to taste, and which she swore was a cure for the gout—something Sweeney has yet to complain of, but, as the woman said in her handwritten letter, what with his rich habits of food and wine, it is "really only a matter of time."

Such random acts of human kindness work against despair, and I began to search my own experience and expertise, if not for a cure then for some remission with my dear friend's name on it.

THERE IS NOTHING LIKE the sight of a dead human body to assist the living in separating the good days from the bad ones. Of this truth I have some experience.

Many's the day I would awaken in gloom—a darkness left over from a dream or the night's drinking or a dread of the day I was awakening to. The moments spent before the mirror while tending to my toilet did nothing to lessen the lessons that Time is certainly not on our side, nor does it heal more wounds than it opens. The ever-retreating hairline, the whitening of one's beard and mustache, the bleeding gums, the basal cell carcinomas, the boils and blisters and bags under the eyes, the belly gone soft, the withering member, the hemorrhoids and hematomas, the varicosities and local edemas, the puff, the paunch, the wrecked version of one's former self that presents itself most mornings, are enough to render most sane men suicidal. And whilst a fresh shave, a dose of toilet water *pour homme*, a pressed suit, new shirt and knatty tie, added to a cup of coffee and a toasted bagel, might quicken in us the will to live, it falls well short of a *joie de vivre*. And many's the morning I would leave home for the long walk across the street to my office at the funeral home bearing the gloom with the round shoulders of the sluggard and poltroon, waiting for the worst to happen.

It was there, in the parlors of the funeral home—my daily stations with the local lately dead—that the darkness would often give way to light. A fellow citizen outstretched in his casket, surrounded by floral tributes, waiting for the homages and obsequies, would speak to me in the silent code of the dead: "So, *you* think *you're* having a bad day?"

The gloom would lift, inexplicably. Here was one to whom the worst had happened, often in a variety of ways, and yet no word of complaint was heard from out the corpse. Nor did the world end, nor the sky fall, nor his or her people become blighted entirely. Life, it turns out, goes on with or without us. All is well. There is at least as much to be thankful for as wary of.

It was thus the balm of my daily witness of mortality and vitality that led me to the course of action that I believed would relieve Matthew Sweeney of much of what he imagined ailed him.

It was to the firm of A. France & Son Undertakers in Lamb's Conduit Street, just around the corner from the Sweeney residence in Holborn, and to Bernard France, proprietor, in particular, that I made application on my pal's behalf. Mr. France, like any undertaker, makes it his business to know his neighbors, a task made easier when the neighbor is a poet of high and wide repute.

So the name of Sweeney was well known to France; and some lines of the former's verse were known by the latter. When I assigned to the name the figure of the man who, in greatcoat and trilby hat, most days in the forenoon would pass by the France shopfront en route to his local for a bottle of Holsten Pils and shepherd's pie, at the bottom of Lamb's Conduit Street, Mr. France agreed, without reservation, that a man of such carriage, such evident good bearing and breeding, could be employed on a full- or part-time basis as a mortuary assistant. That he was possessed of a good black linen suit, matching shoes, an empathetic posture and good personal hygiene, never mind that he was a highly regarded man of letters, all added to Mr. France's enthusiasm at the prospect of Mr. Sweeney "coming on board." He was even willing to overlook the fact that Matthew does not drive—his wariness about entanglements with metal making automobility impossible. His "people skills," as Mr. France called them, would more than compensate. The generous hourly wage he proffered, through my proxy, was a bonus when I considered the medicament that working with the dead would provide for Sweeney's hypochondria.

But when I broached the topic to Himself in Brasserie du Coin, across the street from the mortuary, when I said I'd organized a day job with flexible hours, vacation pay and life insurance with the neighborhood undertaker, there came about his visage such a pallor, it made me think he was about to faint. That the firm had buried Lord Nelson and several other luminaries, ancient and modern, made no difference at all.

"Have ye been banged with a three-wood?" Sweeney cried. "I'd sooner take up day work with dung beetles than work for France." His eyes rolled skyward. He began to swoon. "Oh no no no no no!" He was slipping into his own hellish visions of disorder and corpses and could countenance no further discussion on the matter. I wetted a napkin with cold water, which he applied to his temples and eye sockets. I said no more. Only a meal of lamb shank and smashed celeriac and several glasses of the house red, followed by an espresso and a grappa, restored him to anything like his usual humor.

Mr. France, to his perpetual credit, required no explanation for the rebuff of his tender. I simply told him Mr. Sweeney was "traveling too much" with his literary duties and was "out of sorts." No doubt he dismissed the matter, without prejudice, to artistic sensibilities, making known in no uncertain terms that with regard to Mr. Sweeney, his was a "standing offer." Sensing perhaps my embarrassment, he asked me, as a professional courtesy, to consult on the rapid putrefaction of a body that had come from Majorca the day before—"they've no good embalmers over there"—and to inspect his inventory of coffins and urns, and sent me on my way after tea in his offices with an open invitation to return.

So neither the kindness of strangers nor the connivance of friends, neither science nor superstition, medicine nor academe, government nor religious intervention, could budge the stubborn hypochondria.

HOW IS IT, THEN, that I can here report, in response to the many inquiries, that Matthew Sweeney is not only well, he is better than well—he is in the best form of his adult life, at the top of his game in all ways, so unmistakably in his prime that were he any better he'd be dangerous. This past year alone he has traveled to India without fear of the water, South Africa without fear of the plague, Berlin without fear of the anaerobic bacteria in the hops and barley, America without fear of random violence, Latvia without fear of the women and all over England and Scotland and Wales without fear of the local pestilentia—flesh-eating viruses, infestations of intestines and other outrages reported in the headlines of the evening papers.

Like so much that is wondrous and benign these days, the name of Bill Gates is implicated.

It is to a feast of assorted cheeses from Neals Yard in Covent Garden that I trace the tendrils of Matthew's remission. We were assembled in the publisher's flat in Morwell Street off Bedford Square, my home away from home when I'm in London. We were planning for a joint reading of our poems that was scheduled for that evening in a local venue. I was making program notes on my laptop computer. Matthew had been to the cheesemongers and bakery and off-license and was commenting on the transcendent pleasures that proceeded from coupling the right selection of *fromage* to the correct bottle of wine. He was saying that no computer could come up with the serendipitous configurations of, say, an Isle of Mull Cheddar, a goat from Cork, an elegant Lancashire, a loaf of sourdough and a bottle of decent St. Emillion.

Being teetotal these several years, I could not speak from recent empiricals, but allowed as how quite likely a computer could. In fact, I speculated, it was highly probable that, even as we spoke, Bill Gates had a roomful of foodies tucked away at headquarters in Redmond, Washington, working on software for every culinary contingency. Which glaze with boar's loin, the best garnish with buffalo, all the pesto and pasta and noodle intrigues. Sweeney was squinting in disbelief. What's more, I continued, what could be done for cookery had, in fact, been done for health care. Software was available with medical dictionaries, home cures, symptomatology for the layman for diagnoses, prognoses, treatments and care. His jaw dropped. "Say it isn't so," he said. He had a few goes at my laptop version of Microsoft Golf. I mentioned Internet access to the Poetry Society on both sides of the Atlantic, Web sites for Heaney and Hughes and Yeats, the wonders of email and digital imaging, home banking, word processing, desktop publishing. But it was when I showed him how one search engine would get him from Kafka's grave to Tom Waits's tour schedule in a matter of mouse clicks that Mr. Sweeney went over the edge. His wife and children had long been lobbying for a home computer and now he could see the wisdom in it. He asked if I would help him make the deal.

We stepped out into the daylight of Tottenham Court Road, just north of Oxford Street, where the high-tech shops are bulging with electronic marvels. There was detailed talk about gigabytes and modem speeds, hard drives and preinstalled software, monitors and parallel ports. Matthew assumed the same air of unfocused detachment as one does when another language is being spoken; as I do when he is ordering dim sum. His confidence in me was touching. When it was done he produced a credit card and his particulars for delivery. The salesperson, a very helpful East Indian, took the card and, as salespeople do, asked if Matthew wanted to purchase a maintenance insurance policy. I shook my head. Matthew declined. Perhaps the latest version of Encarta? They were offering a special price, great for the children, homework and all. I shook my head again. Matthew declined. Perhaps an antivirus program? At once Matthew's right eyebrow arched, his back straightened, his eyes widened, focused, rapturous. He breathed deeply.

"They get viruses?" Matthew whispered.

"Oh, yes," the young Calcuttan said. "They're everywhere."

"Yes, antivirus, then, your very best." Matthew never hesitated.

OVER THE NEXT SEVERAL MONTHS, the strangest miracle took place in Dombey Street. Sweeney's concern for the well-being of his computer overwhelmed his worries about his own condition. He ran a daily scan of his disk drive, installed first one diagnostics program, then another. His wife, Rosemary, gave him an upgraded antivirus program for Christmas. His daughter, Nico, found one called "Bug Be Gone" for Father's Day. His son, Malvin, downloaded several beta versions from a Web site on the Internet. In time the prophylactic softwares ate up most of his system's resources. He bought programs to compact memory and uninstall unnecessary programs. Eventually the Calcuttan was called. He came by, took a look at the system and declared that it had the technical equivalent of congestive heart failure. At his suggestion, Matthew added a zip drive, then another, as a kind of bypass surgery. It was mostly the cure that was killing the thing. Apart from the word processor, which housed a new collection of poems, workshop syllabi, various reviews, there was nothing on it but pre-cautionary software. The computer labored on courageously without complaint. If it froze up Matthew would apply an emergency command of CONTROL ALT DELETE, again and again, like the paddles they use when they shout "Clear" on *ER*, until it would restart itself and reboot its programs. Sweeney's emails were full of warnings about the latest virus, the evildoings of hackers and brainiacs, who attached them to files and mailed them out to unsuspecting clients such as we.

And all the while he was feeling better. Gone from his correspondence were his worries over something he ate, or not enough sleep, or the airborne pathogens in public transit. Silenced were his habitual concerns about contagions, impactions, tachycardia and cysts. These were replaced by a very tender bedside manner— in fact, he kept the computer in his bedroom—adopted with regard to the precarious condition of his patient.

When he first read about the Millennium Bug in *The Evening Standard*, rather than panic he assumed the calm resolution that the kin of terminal cases do. He accepted the inevitable and began to plan for the big crash at midnight on the eve of 2000.

As of this writing there's no telling what might happen. Whether Y2K is doom or deliverance, Sweeney is certain he shouldn't be alone. Nor will he be caught unawares. Prearrangements are under way for a New Year's send-off or celebration—a very special gathering in Dombey Street. The guest list is rumored to include the senior editors of the best U.K. publishing houses, at least one Irish Nobel Prize winner, the Scotswoman who might have been named poet laureate had her poems and her sexual preferences been less remarkable, the staff from Neals Yard who sing barbershop, remarkably, in a quartet they call Curds and Whey; and because the worst is always on the verge of happening, the Calcuttan from Tottenham Court Road, who has promised a plate of his wife's vindaloo, and Bernard France from A. France & Son, whose offices, like all peril and possibility, are just around the corner.

Bible Studies

I t is always a choice between the soft-porn movies and the Gideon's Bible. Killing time in posh hotels fills me with thoughts of nakedness and peril and the salvation of my soul. Perhaps I'm in need of professional help, nearing the end of a three-week indenture to my publishers—days divided between radio blather, chitchat with the local papers and evening readings in bookstores, where one competes with the din of commerce and cappuccino to peddle books with one's name on them. There's the night's sleep and the ship-out to the airport in the early o'clock, the intense flattery of perfect strangers reading something I've written and the labor-intensive blur of well-intentioned, well-meaning, well-spoken people whom I regret I will likely never see again. Not root canal, to be sure; neither the glamour and glory envisioned when they first broached the topic of a national tour.

I could be back home directing funerals.

To her permanent credit, the publicist back in Manhattan always puts me up in good hotels—ones that neither overwhelm in

the lobby nor disappoint upstairs. She is twentyish, brunette, bookish and lovely and crazy in love with a man who works night shifts
at the SoHo Grand. She knows from safe lodging and holy rest.
From her windowless cubicle across from the editor's corner
office, she imagines the romance of a life on the road—the nakedness, the peril, the salvation of her soul—the balm of leisure and
creature comforts. Which might be why I always end up in places
where I miss my wife all the more for the king-sized beds, the intimate dining available downstairs, the tiled baths abundant with
unguents and powders and perfumed soaps, the cushy towels, the
Jacuzzi and tanning lamps and honor bar full of chocolates and
cheeses and bottled aphrodisiacs. I rummage among the comforts
for the ones you do solo. I locate the data port, savor the mint on
the pillow. It is not meet for man to be alone.

Our text is taken from the Book of Genesis.

Sometimes I wonder why it is we die.

Near as I can figure it has to do with Sex. It is the sword and
sheath we live and die by: We're dying for it and because of it. The
arithmetic of divisible resources of time and space leave us finite
answers. Whether causal, casual or coincidental, sex and death are
difficult twins. They nearly rhyme. Both leave you wide-eyed,
blinking back your disbelief, out of breath, fumbling for a cigarette
and something to say. Both bring you face-to-face with your maker.
Both are horizontal mysteries. Both make you think you should
have spent more time on your knees. Both are over before you
know it. Both are biblical. Read the first few chapters. You can try
this at home.

"In the beginning" is how it always begins.

There's the Garden of Eden and the Tree of Knowledge and

the Voice of God booming out of the darkness. He's already spent a week on the prelims—birds of the air, fishes of the sea, beasts of the field and forests and plants—the basics of biology and geography and the food chain. The First Guy is made in God's own image and likeness from the mud of the earth. And God, wanting Adam to feel masterly, wanting to prop up his apparently fragile male ego, brings all the other creatures to him for naming. Thus, from the noisy void, the first orderly syllables are assigned: *orangutan, rock bass, titmouse, magnolia.* This is good duty, he's using his index finger. *Brown trout, watermelon, goldfinch, goat.* He's beginning to think that he knows what he's doing. *Yellow jacket, winter oak, polar bear.* He's really feeling much better about himself. *Big Dipper, sweet potato, Euphrates.* But nothing among the things he names subtracts from Adam's essential loneliness, neither *bison* nor *kumquat* nor *python* nor *rose.* He fancies none of them. He is alone.

It is then, in the twenty-first verse of chapter 2 of the Book of Genesis, that "God caused a deep sleep to fall upon the man." From a rib removed from Adam's side, a helpmate is fashioned. He wakes and finds her. He approves. "At last, bone of my bones, flesh of my flesh; this one shall be called Woman"—not Shakespeare, but, all the same, it is a touching moment in every translation. They are naked and unashamed, they are lovely and immortal. There is nothing in their touching but love and comfort. This is why they call the place Paradise.

Now the details of the Fall—how we came to be mortal—are all reported in chapter three and are largely undisputed. There's this talking snake who is very cunning and convinces the woman that the fruit on the tree in the middle of the garden will give them whatever it is they seem to be missing—and what's missing? This is an intensely womanly question; one by which all history and commerce is shaped. They're barenaked, the weather is perfect, there's plenty of food, no death or taxes or credit-card debt; the beasts won't bite them because it's Paradise. They want for nothing because they *want for nothing*.

Only thing is, their coupling is a little lackluster—a kind of brute beast biologic elective, short on foreplay and afterglow. They're not going to die, so why bother breeding? There's an endless supply and thus little demand. They are innocent and ignorant and full of bliss. What's missing, of course, is Heartache & Desire, Lust & Wonder, Need & Sweet Misery, Love & Grief—all the passionate derivatives of Sex and Death that any woman in her right mind knows the world really needs if there's going to be progress. And so when she eats of the fruit of the tree of knowledge and convinces her Adam that he should do the same, the knowledge they get is the knowledge of good and evil, the facts of the matter of human nature—we want, we hurt and hunger, we thirst and crave, we weep and laugh, dance and desire, more and more and more. We only do these things because we die. We only die because we do these things. The fruit of the tree in the middle of Eden, being forbidden, is sexy and tempting, tasty and fatal.

The Fall of Man and Free Market Capitalism, no less the doctrines of Redemptive Suffering and Supply and Demand, are based on the notion that enough is never enough. And ever since Eden, it never has been. Every covenant of blood and plunder since—from circumcision and crucifixion to rape and pillage, bull markets and leveraged buyouts—has been based on the axiom, intuited by Eve, that no one pays for cows where milk is free. A world of carnal bounty and commercial indifference where men and women have no private parts, nor shame nor guilt nor fear of death, would never evolve into a place that Darwin and Bill Gates and the Dalai Lama could be proud of. They bit the apple and were banished from it.

The first thing, of course, is they notice they're naked. Size immediately begins to matter. And privacy. This is the beginning of the fashion trade—from fig leaves and loincloths to Calvin Klein and Kate Moss, the way we cover ourselves is based on the quietly erotic notions of how we might uncover each other. Suddenly Adam and Eve can't get enough. Not two verses later they are making Cain and Abel, from whom we learn competition and the killing instincts so important to hunters and gatherers and CEOs. There are the pains of her childbirth and the sweat of his brow: labor and work ethics and wages of sin from whence proceed maternity leave, childcare and gender politics, turf wars and serfdom, slavery and soybean futures, chattel and sexual harassment law. Every civilizing impulse and invention, likewise every savagery—from animal husbandry to lawn tennis, flush toilets to palliative care, democracy to despotism, papal infallibility to the Chevrolet—proceeds from that banishment from Eden and our efforts to replicate and return to a place where we were satisfied, sufficient, at one with the immortals of creation.

Walk through any High Street or mall or international airport and consider the enterprises that would not be there if not for sex and death—our hunger for one and horror at the other. Would we bother with jewelers or florists or Victoria's Secrets, homeopathy or cellular phones, condoms or tummy tucks, sushi or wine bars, churches, estate planners or actuarials? If not for the grim reaper, would we need rabbis or shamans, priests or ayatollahs, senators or software, Pooh Bahs, potentates, 401Ks? Would we marry or bury or baptize or burn? Would we buy insurance, aftershave, laptops or toasters? If we never took notice of each other's nakedness, would sit-ups or Nikes or surgeries that augment or reduce or uplift be the vogue? Would there be much of a market in Web browsers, junk bonds, Prozac, headstones, self-help or psychotherapy if we weren't all dying and in search of love? If everyone always had enough, would we bother with world wars or Wall Street or the Super Bowl? Would we have bothered with the Magna Carta, the Cultural Revolution, the Renaissance or the Reformation, the military-industrial complex? If Hitler or Nixon or Maggie Thatcher, Catherine of Siena or William the Conqueror, Vince Lombardi or Genghis Khan, Pope Adrian or Joan of Arc, Bill Clinton or Mick Jagger, been "satisfied," you know, sexually, emotionally, psychosocially, would they have risen or fallen to their heights and depths? Would we worry, disabused of our carnal concerns or mortality issues, over eco-terrorism, Viagra or Wonder Bras, germ warfare or the NASDAQ or our self-esteem? Would we have any interest in Big Berthas, Little Caesars, exit polls or income tax? Would there be any history, economy or body politic? "Imagine," to borrow John Lennon's sensible directive, "there's no hunger."

So next time you're lounging about in your Tommy Hilfigers puffing on a Habano Primero, considering the well-being of your no-load mutuals or the good fortune of having a dream house and trophy spouse and designer problems, thank neither God nor your broker nor the hunch you had. Thank neither your hypnotist nor personal trainer nor the blonde in your support group. Thank Eve, the Mother of the Marketplace, the Patroness of Necessity and Invention, Madonna of Desire and Mortality, without whose hankering for forbidden fruits we'd all have remained tabulae rasae, ignorant, blissful, naked and shameless, wanting for nothing, neither soft porn nor Gideons, room service or frequent flyer miles, a species of the unemployed and unencumbered, ne'er-do-wells and ne'er-do-harms, sitting around in our all-togethers grinning for no apparent reason, humming cantatas, reciting sonnets, touching each other with the unspeakable tenderness of heaven, blessed and elect and bored to tears, forever and ever, world without end, Amen.

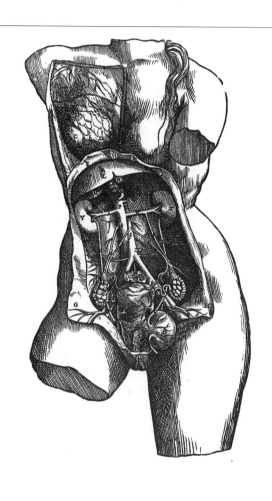

W o m b s

The contemplation of the womb, like staring into the starlit heavens, fills me with images of Somethingness or Nothingness. It was ever thus. If space is the final frontier, the womb is the first one—that place where, to borrow Wallace Stevens's phrase, the idea of the thing becomes the thing itself. It is the tabernacle of our expectations. The safe haven we are ever longing to replicate in our latter-day habitats. A place where the temps are set, the rent is cheap, the food is good and we aren't bothered by telephones or the tax man. That space we are born out of, into this world, where the soft iambics of our mother's heart become the first sure verses of our being.

My mother taught me to say my prayers. I learned the Hail Mary in two languages, neither of which made any sense to me. I could sing it in Latin, angelic in my ignorance. But I said it over and over in English all through the days of my youth, encouraged first by my mother, then by the blue nuns who schooled me as a boy in the rubrics of Catholicism. It was where I first heard any mention of wombs. The rosary taught us to say them quickly—fifty of them, with a sprinkling of Our Father's and Glory Be's—letting the words blur into glorious or sorrowful mysteries, Zen-like, a mantra for ritual mourning, family devotions, private meditations. But late at night I would linger over the syllables, pondering the imponderable meanings, and study the sense as well as the sound: "Blessed art thou amongst women and blessed is the fruit of thy womb Jesus." This struck me as a strange benediction. Did Jesus have a womb? Was I missing a comma, a colon, a period?

It was early October 1958. I was nine, about to be ten. Pope Pius XII was dying in Italy. I was listening to the radio and saying my rosary, staring out of the window into the night sky and wondering about wombs. The prayer observed the circumstances surrounding the birth of Jesus. It was first among the several stories we were taught by the nuns that had a decidedly sexual subtext. Here's what happened: a young Jewish woman, pledged in troth to a local carpenter, was minding her business, saying her prayers, when the angel of the Lord appeared to her and gave out with the words that named this prayer, to wit, Hail Mary! Then, after the customary pleasantries, she was given to believe that she would soon find herself to be with child. This, she told the angel, was impossible, as she and Joseph, good Jews that they were, had kept a cleanly distance in their courtship. Not to worry, said the angel, the Holy Ghost would impregnate her. No less a force than the Power of the Most High would overshadow her, and the fruit of this union would be called the Son of God. This is Luke's version of it. Matthew reports a dream of Joseph's, Mary's cuckolded betrothed, who falls asleep much troubled by her apparent changes. An angel appears in his dream and explains that she hasn't been unfaithful—it was the Holy Spirit that filled her womb.

"C'est le pigeon, Joseph," as James Joyce retells the French folktale in his great *Ulysses*—"It was the dove," the blessed virgin tells the carpenter. So here was the Remarkable Conception.

Then, as now, the church seemed to have an inordinate interest in the private lives and private parts of women. The high value placed on virginity was coincidental with an enthusiasm for fertility. That these seemed at cross-purposes was one of the several mysteries of a nunnish boyhood and my devoutly lapsed adulthood.

But I recall clearly that it was sometime in 1958, watching my mother grow large with the pregnancy that would become my sister Julie Ann, and praying the rosary for the dying pope, that I began what would become a lifelong interest in the womb. There'd been five of us before Julie Ann, and there'd be three more to follow before our folks were through, but it was the autumn of 1958, a year after the Russians launched Sputniks I and II, that the womb became the wonder of my world.

I'd seen an episode of *Playhouse 90*—a mid-century TV show—whilst spending the night at a friend's house, that portrayed the plight of unwed mothers. This formed in me the earliest curiosities about procreation. At ten I reckoned that marriage was the cause of pregnancy because folks got married and then had babies. That this seemed the natural order of things testifies to the protected environment in which I was reared. My mother was having babies all the years of my youth. Of nine of us, I was number two. The youngest of my siblings was born when I was sixteen, by which time I had sorted out the relations between men and women and their babies.

It was after the *Playhouse 90* piece that I began asking questions of my mother about how someone got to be a mother without being wed. She spoke to me in her ordinary voice about love and desire, how God gave parents the pleasure of each other's company as a way of making babies, how it involved the dearest and nearest of embraces between my father and her and that someday I would meet someone I would love so much that I would want to hold that way and that I would be a good husband and a good father to my children because I had what she called a good heart. She told me that this embrace, this *intercourse*, was so very pleasurable that men and women who loved one another loved to hold each other in just this way as often as they could. And the pleasure, she told me, was a gift from God given by nature as a kind of compensation for the duties and responsibilities of parenthood that inevitably and naturally followed. Children were precious and birth was a miracle and she and my father felt blessed to be part of God's plan. She held my face between her hands, she kissed me, she smiled, she returned to the ironing.

Then I asked Sister Jean Thérèse. I was twelve by now and admiring the breasts of girls in school and trying to figure out a way to get my hands on them and spending a lot of time alone in my room contemplating the mysteries of the universe and some magazines that Jimmy Shroeder and I found stashed in his basement under the stairs.

Sister Jean Thérèse had wonderful breasts as well, though the black and blue habits of her order of nuns—the Immaculate Heart of Mary, IHM's—made every effort to hide them. She was very pleased that I had asked her about these things and made no secret of that fact that the Facts of Life were better learned from her than from the boyos who hung out on the corner. And though

I had never seen these fellows, and didn't know exactly which corner she was talking about, I made a mental note to search them out as soon as I was able. She explained to me in sensible detail the biology and physiology of reproduction, sexual attraction, the morality of the calling to married life. She articulated the proper names of parts and processes I'd never heard of before. *Conjugal* and *uterus* and *semen* and *penis* were spoken with the same weighty precision as my mother had uttered *intercourse*. She told me that men must assume responsibility for their behavior toward women. She said that sex was the most intimate language and that to speak such intimacies to someone we did not love was a little like speaking English to someone who knew only French. Eventually it would make no sense. Love, Sister Jean Thérèse said, was the cipher, the code, that made sex make sense. And sex, she said, was a gift of God to help true lovers understand each other. She carried on with metaphors and images in hushed and breathless tones until, flush with what I figured was the Holy Ghost, she asked me if I had any questions. I was dumbstruck by the beauty of her breasts and intellections. She smiled warmly, much relieved, clearly pleased that she had passed this test with me. A holy woman in her twenties, a virgin bride of Christ, she pulled me to herself and hugged me—my face buried deep in the space between her breasts, my cheek pressed against the heavy crucifix her order wore—I was not scarred for life but was, ever after that, a fool for love.

For his part, my father added to my tutelage thus. I'd gotten some glossy girlie mags from those boyos on the corner and made a pact with my brothers Dan and Pat to stash them in the attic space behind our bedroom walls. There they were discovered by my father during his weekly patrols. These were the years before children got quality time and their own space in trade for their parents' time and interest in their lives. We assumed no right to privacy. He didn't trust our willingness to go to bed at night, our sudden interest in homework, the number of naps we claimed to be taking. He interrogated us as to their ownership. We all sang dumb, feigning wonder and innocence. He said he'd give them to our uncle Pat, who served in the local police department, to have the fingerprints lifted. If we wouldn't fess up, he'd get to the bottom of this. These were the days of Eliot Ness and *The Untouchables,* and we brothers knew the long arm of the law could reach us. But we held our ground and worried for a week, then another. Dan got a rash, Pat turned insomniac, I thought maybe I ought to see a priest. When would the damning results come back from the lab? They never did. I remember only my father's forgiveness, albeit weeks later, fishing for bluegill on Orchard Lake, his quiet assurance that such curiosities, though normal, were better indulged in other ways. And his insistence that such magazines showed disrespect for our mother and sisters and would not be tolerated in his house. "Women are not just parts," he told us, "they are someone's daughters or sisters or mothers or wives."

So I owe to my mother and the nuns and my ever-vigilant father my earliest understandings, however biased and beatified they were, of the mysteries of life. They conspired to establish in my psyche indelibly the elemental connections between and among love and sex and nativity. These connections might be causal or correlated or coincidental. Folks might make love for the pleasure of sex, or have sex as a token of love, or have babies as emblems of love or as a consequence of sex. But these three things, love and sex and parenthood, were related. And the people who

shared them were likewise related by blood or bliss or love or
memory. More years later than I like to admit, the memorable
pleasures of my clumsy first couplings were sharpened by the wariness I'd carried since watching *Playhouse 90* that there might be
some life-changing consequence of such behavior. It might leave
us lovesick or disillusioned or with child. It might mean everything
or nothing at all. But once touched by a lover with such approval,
I knew I would never be the same.

Of course, the lessons of my experience, and the culture at
large, include the ones that seek to disassociate these pieces of
life's puzzle. Sex is frequently and fervently practiced absent love.
"Free love" we called it in the sixties, as if by saying it we could
make it so. And babies are no longer the natural outcome of our
couplings. More often they are reckoned a lapse in planning. Love
or reproduction are less often the prime motives. On the contrary,
pleasure is preeminent. "If you can't be with the one you love,
honey, / Love the one you're with." This was fairly easy duty. And,
though it is true that I was passionately attached to my first sexual
partners, and feel nothing but fondness toward them decades
since, it was not love—I know it now, having known love since. We
can, it turns out, disentangle the mélange of meaning and performance and outcomes. We can have love without sex, sex without
love and both without babies, which we may acquire lovelessly and
sexlessly in a lab. We may, against my father's counsel, think of each
other in terms of parts. And I often wonder whether I should count
it a curse or a blessing that I came of age in an age when the reproductive choices of the species were expanding, just as its explo-
rations of space were expanding. The personal was becoming
politicized. We stared into outer space and reasoned there must be

life. We stared into the womb and proclaimed it must be something else. Men and women have made it to the moon, but we see ourselves as creatures from different planets.

But just as outer space has been colonized, commercialized and politicized by late-century technologies, the womb, first among our species' inner spaces, has been likewise exposed, explored and exploited by invasive interests. So-called feminists, so-called Christians, so-called welfare reformers and social scientists have all staked their claims to the uses and abuses of its miracles. Bishops and abortionists—advocates on either side, true believers all—talk less and take sides more. Of all the existential questions asked of my generation, none has been more divisive than the ones about the womb—whose it is, what's in there, who gets to say what goes on with it. The borders of our reproductive lives have been blurred by a technology and a body politic that seem at odds. The starlit heavens have been easier to sort. Research may have dampened the romance, but by staring into space we have produced some global courtesies about space stations and star wars. Considering the larger universe, our national interests pale in favor of a larger citizenship. But the study of the womb, the arts and sciences of procreation, has disabused us of some precious mythologies. It has given us options more quickly than it has given us clues about the ethical, moral and practical implications. We are driven from the sweet expectant talk between parents and lovers into the polemics of planned parenthood and gender wars waged over life and choice, over the social, scientific, economic and political province of the womb.

• • •

To be pro-life one must be a radical Christian—a Republican or a papist or a Baptist or a sexist brute who wants to impose his personal morality on the culture at large, already suffering from patriarchy, and unwanted children, and abandoned welfare mothers, and talk-radio extremists. It's okay, the argument goes, for one to regard abortion as evil "for one's self," just don't try to limit everyone's choice.

To be pro-choice one must be a radical feminist, a left-leaning liberal, a godless social engineer working toward the dissolution of the family and of family values. Why worry about unborn whales if unborn humans are no more than "the products of conception"? If the lives of the unborn, the pro-lifers argue, cannot be protected from the baby killers, who among us is ever safe?

I have a daughter and three sons. I'm in favor of life, and in favor of choice. Life is not easy. Either is choice. My daughter and sons are biologically prepared and equipped for reproduction. Here are their choices as I see them. Each can choose whether or not, with whom and where, when and why, to be sexually active. They can choose how much or how little meaning it has, how much or how little of themselves to invest. Each can choose what, if any, precaution to take against disease and pregnancy. And should such precautions fail to protect—if they become diseased or impregnated—each has the choice either to live with the consequences or to take their leaves. But if they choose to live, the available choices, up till now commensurate, take different directions according to gender lines.

My daughter, finding herself with an unplanned pregnancy, may choose to have the baby with or without the consent, cooperation, or co-parenting of the fellow (shall we call him the father now?) who impregnated her. Or she may choose, in light of her life's circumstances, that a child would be terribly inconvenient, and she may avail herself of what the courts have declared is her constitutionally guaranteed right to a safe and legal medical procedure that would terminate her pregnancy, void her maternity, abort the viability of whatever it is inside her womb. No permission or approval is necessary beyond her willingness to exercise her choice. Whatever discomfort—moral or personal or maternal— she might feel would do nothing to change the fact that she would have acted within her constitutional rights. A pregnancy that results from bilateral consent is legally undone by unilateral choice. *Our Bodies, Ourselves,* the doctrine goes. If we uphold my daughter's choice in the matter, we are said to be pro-choice. If we consider the contents of her womb to have a life and interest of its own and that my daughter's choices end where those interests begin, we are said to be pro-life. Either way, we get to choose which team we're on, which side we take, which sign to carry in the endless debate.

But if reproductive choice—the choice as to when one is ready, willing and able to parent—is a good thing, wouldn't it be good for my sons as well? And if that choice may be exercised after conception, as it currently is by women, then shouldn't men have the same option: to proclaim, legally and unilaterally, the end of their interest in the tissue or fetus or baby (depending on one's team affiliations) or whatever it is that sex between a man and a woman sometimes produces. As it stands now, paternity, once determined, means fiscal responsibility for eighteen years, according to law. There is currently, for my sons, no choice in the matter.

If one of them impregnates a woman and the woman chooses to have the child, she has a legal claim against the income of the father. He may, of course, refuse to pay, refuse his paternity, in which case he would be a "deadbeat dad," or some other media-made word for "no good." But if their sister can choose, unilaterally, to void her maternity and abort her parental role as a matter of a constitutionally protected choice, why oughtn't my sons have an equivalent choice—say, within the first two trimesters—to declare their decision not to parent, to void their paternity, whatever the impregnated woman does notwithstanding? Isn't this precisely the same choice given to women by *Roe* v. *Wade* and laws elsewhere that uphold this "right"?

But pregnancy and abortion, some several will argue, are women's issues, a woman's body. "It's none of your business" I am sometimes told. "Once men can get pregnant, then you can talk!" Is it really all about wombs, then? Is biology destiny, after all? As if condoms, the ones that fit on men's penises, are none of any woman's business. Or, since only my sons are required to register with Selective Service, their sister should be kept from the discussions of war, or foreign policy, or defense spending. When someone is kept from the conversation because of their body parts, shall we call it sexism or affirmative action?

Of course, the young men of my generation were quite willing to leave this a woman's issue. We had learned from our fathers and our mothers that babies—before, during and after their births—were mostly women's issues. The conventional image of expectant fatherhood involved a handful of cigars, a helpless vigil in a waiting room while the mother was in "labor." Then she would go home to her duties and he would leave home for his—his labor.

Hers was to nurture and educate, his was to protect and pay. It was so for Lucy and Ricky, Ward and June. Father knew best and mother stayed home with the babies. Young men died in wars, young women in childbirth. Old men died first. Old women died later, too often alone.

The division of labor was sane and sensible. The division of power, economic and political, of course, was not. Mid-century feminists identified the links between the womb and this imbalance. Tied to their children by a lifelong umbilicus, tied to their home fires by their indenture to the family, they could not travel light and fast like men, who climbed the postwar corporate ladders, owned cars, wrote checks, ran the country. The oral contraceptive provided the first line of defense against the encumbrances of maternity. Abortion rights became the fail-safe. And the first waves of rapidly shifting gender politics that made landfall in the sixties and seventies instructed men of my generation that to question women on such issues would assure a lonely life. To get a little, in the parlance of our youth, we had to get along. Besides, we were only too willing to approve—sex without babies was a delightful concept. Freed from the worry of pregnancy, women could relax and think about pleasure—ours and theirs. And pleasure, we found out, was portable and modular. Love was nice, but in a pinch, pleasure would do. Talk turned to climax and clitorises, orgies and orgasms, G-spots and casual, instead of causal, sex. The intimate lexicons of sex, formerly meaningful because of their potential consequences, seemed, for a few years in the sixties and seventies, "duty-free." It was an illusion, but a sweet one.

And men of my generation were quite pleased to have the dutiful business of reproductive life worked out in a deal struck by earnest, rightfully angry women and the lawyerly old men on the

Supreme Court. In 1973 the name given to this deal was *Roe* v. *Wade*. Women saw it as freedom from the constraints imposed by their wombs, their rightful ownership of their lives and bodies. Men saw it as pretty much none of their business.

Still, if women wanted access to the offices and factories, men made their way into birthing rooms and nurseries. Inevitably, difficult questions arose.

Is it the species or the gender that reproduces? Aren't pregnancy and parenting human issues? I know they were when my sons and daughter were "expected." Their mother was "expecting." So was I. And while a woman's body is certainly involved in her maternity, a man's is involved in his paternity. Women may choose legally to evict the fetus from their wombs because their right to privacy includes dominion over their bodies and the bodies inside of them. But do we not ask men for eighteen years of work and toil, their body's "labor," in support of the babies born of their loins? If they refuse, which too many do, we do not call it a privacy issue, we call them scoundrels. The former is optional, the latter is required by current law.

And though I am encouraged and inclined to march in favor of a woman's right to choose a safe, legal and affordable medical procedure to abort her maternity, where are the women who will march with me to uphold the rights of my sons and their sons in the matter—to choose a safe, legal and affordable legal procedure to terminate, for reasons that range from good to not so good, their paternity? Is Choice good for one and *all* or only one and *half* of the population?

"If they don't want the responsibility, they should keep their pants on!" is what I am told by several women of my acquaintance. Truth told, it sounds like sound advice. But the same advice, tendered to my daughter or to the daughters of my women friends, is regarded as suspect, sexist, patriarchal. "If you don't want the responsibility, you should keep your panties on." "You've made your bed, now lie in it!" "If you're going to dance, you've got to pay the piper."

"You just don't *get it*," is how it usually ends.

Is it possible that the choices now legally available to women with regard to their reproductive lives, when considered for men, seem irresponsible, overly indulgent, selfish and sexist and ultimately contrary to the best interests of the species?

What would it look like if a million men or so, next year, within twelve weeks of impregnating their sexual partners, were to declare, for reasons they had to articulate to no one, their interest in the fetus null and void, ceased and aborted? What if there were clinics, operated by Planned Parenthood, or a benign nonprofit, where the paperwork could be conducted cleanly for a reasonable fee—these paper "procedures" done by lawyers instead of doctors, assisted by paralegals instead of nurses, the deliverance safe, legal, unilateral, constitutionally protected, the same for the fathers as for mothers? Would protesters march in front of such clinics? Would signs appear calling them unflattering names? Would pictures of destitute children, poor fetuses, abandoned mothers, punctuate these protests? If most of us are, as we are frequently told, pro-choice, oughtn't the courts to uphold this choice as well?

In the past we have watched while the courts decided public policy on life and death. Policies designed to redress exceptional hardships have become the rule. An image we are encouraged to conjure in defense of abortion rights is that of a woman impregnated by rape or incest or at risk of her own life by pregnancy, forced to line up in a back alley where some heartless wretch has at her with a coat hanger. The image is not a fiction. There are painful cases. People died. Something in the system was very wrong.

Twenty-five years later we have abortion on demand, a million and a half of them every year, something less than 5 percent of them performed on victims of rape or incest or women at risk of their very lives. The other 95 percent, presumably, occupy a place on the continuum between what has been called a "life-affirming moral choice" and a bad decision. Either way, thirty-five million since 1973; nearly one third of all pregnancies. There are few legal limits on when or why or whom or how, and any effort to moderate what has become an "open season" is shouted down as a return to the back alley and coat hanger. Many of those of us who favor choice, who uphold the individual's dominion over his or her body, now wonder if the present reality was the one we had in mind. Were there any other available options? To be pro-choice must we tolerate all of the choices, even the worst ones? To be pro-life must we tolerate all of our lives? This is a difficult math to do.

The politics of the womb, like the politics of space, involve not only our public interests but our private ones as well. And in the long-standing debates over the first frontier—who will be born and who willn't—the terrible din of public rhetoric has obscured the talk between fathers and daughters, mothers and sons, brothers and sisters, husbands and wives. We have been driven to the extremes, made noisome caricatures, in a conflict that supports a growing industry of pollsters, politicos, lobbyists and pundits. The rhetoric of the NOW defending late-term abortions sounds like nothing so much as the NRA defending our rights to AK-47's. Slippery slopers of different stripes, they fear the inch that will become the mile. They fear the reasoned, quiet talk between women and men, who see in each other's eyes neither creatures from Mars nor creatures from Venus, but citizens of the same planet, fellow pilgrims, neighbors, lovers, teachers, willing friends.

Women are right to abhor decisions about their bodies that leave them out. So are men. The reproductive life of the species is not a woman's issue. It is a human one. It requires the voices of human beings. And the language it deserves is intimate.

Such voices, such lexicons, were among the early casualties in the gender wars of the last four decades. The hard sciences that have extended our control into space and the womb have taken in trade much of the mystery that informed the heavens and human nature. We have disconnected sexual performance from existential consequence, and in doing so we have become a culture of polarized parts—sperm donors and ovaries—men and women who too seldom see in the faces of their lovers the faces of their children and their children's parents. My daughter and my sons inherit a world in which the mechanics and politics of making love and making babies have been distanced from the meaning of making families. That women have been oppressed is not a secret. Nor is it news that men have been betrayed. We are members of an evolving species, victims and beneficiaries of science and nature. The blaming of mothers for the trouble with sons, like the blaming of husbands for the trouble with wives, can be defended or debunked by the arrangement of facts. But the rebuke keeps us from the deeper meaning of our lives.

One night before my first child was born, I lay in bed beside his mother. She was sleeping. It was late November. We lived in a rented cottage beside a small lake. The night was dark, the stars were bright. In the half-light I could see her belly moving—hands or feet or head, I didn't know. But I knew what occupied her womb was partly me and would change our lives forever. Looking out into the night I spied the dominant winter constellation, Orion, and, just to the right, the Pleiadies—six of the seven sisters plain to see. To name a few out of the countless stars was a comfort. The woman sleeping, the baby bulging in her, the bright and blinking firmament alive, alive—I felt myself at ease on the edge of a new life, full of hope and wonder and thanks. I remember regretting that I would ever die. And remember knowing, for the first time, that I could.

The Bang & Whimper
and the Boom

My son and I were mov-
ing caskets—an oak
with Celtic crosses on
the corners, a cherry with a finish like our dining room table, a
cardboard box with a reinforced bottom—each could be buried,
each could be burned, each could be blown into space or set adrift.
The baby boomers who are buying now do better with a broad
selection. I was talking to my son about "protection"—about condoms and careful choices and coming of age. He'd been out too
late the night before.

Caskets and condoms serve well as late-century emblems of
sex and death, how it is we come and go, the corruptible body's
effort to put on incorruption. Practically speaking, one size fits all,
but existentially they border on the voids between human being
and human ceasing to be.

But my son had heard all of this before. The X his generation
is named for marks the spot where pleasure and peril intersect,
and he and his siblings are experts in these cautionary tales. In a
display room full of caskets and cremation urns, he wants to talk
about his future.

He says he wants to be a funeral director. He wonders if I'd ever sell to one of the huge conglomerates. They're buying up firms like ours across the globe: Frank E. Campbell in Manhattan; Kenyon in London, who used to bury the royals; most everything in Paris; and, closer to home, here in Michigan, they bought out our nearest competition last year. Cash and stock options for his brick and mortar, rolling stock, receivables and the name on the sign. They are banking on the boomer years, the next twenty or thirty, when the death rate will top the ten-per-thousand mark and the number of deaths in the United States will increase by one million every year. The talk inside the trade is that they raise the prices, cut services, centralize the management, push pre-need and after-care sales-ops and pay the shareholders handsomely. Less for more, voice mail and corporate cover, a good rating on the stock exchange—they have become the mortuary version of the American Way.

"The only problem is they buy your name. It's all you really have," I tell my son. The name on the sign—ours says LYNCH & SONS—is the one they call in the middle of the night when there is trouble. It's the one that makes you accountable to the community you live in, the people you live with. It's who can be trusted if the job is done well and who is to blame if ever it's not. We can build new buildings, buy new cars, do a brisk traffic in caskets and cremation urns and vaults and markers, but any damage to the name is permanent. It is the one asset we can't replace and dare not sell. It's an elderly form of consumer protection.

My father taught me about protection. It was the late sixties, early seventies. The planet was perilous and changing. I think he wanted me to "be prepared."

He taught me by role playing. It was all the rage. We'd go into the casket selection room at the funeral home. He'd be the undertaker—no stretch for him. I'd be the bereaved client with the dead mother—pure theater for me. My mother was going strong back then, full of life, still surrounded by my toddling younger siblings. I was floundering between colleges and careers, not quite certain about my "future," interested mostly in Irish poetry and Italian women. I had been to West Clare and to the Continent, back and forth a couple of times, learning to speak with a brogue and to woo dark beauties in the dialects of Venice and the Dolomites.

I worked at the funeral home to finance my travel and indecision. It was a job then, not a living, not a life. I was paid by the hour. I caught the phones at night, slept in the apartment on the second floor, kept my passport handy, my bag packed. I never knew if I was coming or going.

MY FATHER'S INSISTENCE that I learn caskets seemed, in the parlance of my generation, "weird," "bizarre," "far out, man!" A child of those boom years at the confluence of industry and technology, mine was a mind-set of gleaming new products and possibilities. The retail end of the mortuary trade was boring by contrast, a downer indeed—an underworld of macabre and morbid curiosities about which I was anything but curious. What possible interest would a young boomer have in Elgin Permaseals and Wilbert Monticello burial vaults and the adjustable beds of Batesville Monogard caskets? The only adjustable bed I'd any interest in was the one I was sharing, more or less à la carte, with Elena Pascuzzi in the back of her van, Tuesdays and Saturdays— my evenings off. Elena, a bookish woman with admirable bone structure, had read Simone de Beauvoir and Germaine Greer, *The Feminine Mystique* and the voluptuously titled *Our Bodies, Ourselves*. She was a lapsed Catholic, a born-again and braless communicant of the Good News that, thanks to the Mamas and the Papas and the Pill, she would exercise, at will, her right as a woman to initiate sex and enjoy sex out loud and to its fullest and to treat men as equals and sexual objects. This, of course, was fine with me and fine I reckon with the other happy objects of her affections, however fleeting, with whom she field-tested these notions those nights of the week that I was stuck at work. So to have my father rub my nose so deeply in the fact of death at a time when the Facts of Life seemed like so much fun no doubt damaged me in ways I'm only lately recovering the memory of. Surely, some twitch or addiction can be traced to it. Certainly I am permanently scarred. Hadn't Kennedy and Vietnam and the threat of Nuclear Holocaust been sufficient lessons in mortality? Hadn't we boomers bummers enough? For crissakes, where was Oprah when we needed her?

"THE FIRST ONE you show them is very important—it establishes the midrange, the average—you know, not the most expensive and not the least."

I'd already learned never to say "cheap."

My father would stop at the first casket, an eighteen-gauge steel number called the Praying Hands because of the appliqué in the cap panel. He'd lift the velvet overlay to expose the rubber gasket on the edge and, looking earnestly in my eyes, he'd begin.

"The most important difference between one casket and another has to do with its *protective qualities*. Most of the metal caskets in this room are what we call *sealed* caskets, because of this gum-rubber gasket that runs around the perimeter of the casket shell and *seals against air and moisture.*"

Properly impressed with the technical splendor of a casket with a gasket but perplexed at the notion of safety when it came to corpses, I'd get into character readily.

"Who cares," I'd say, acting the doubtful Thomas, "about a *sealed* casket? Who needs it? Anyway, isn't she dead?"

He'd show me the crank used to close the casket, insert it in the end and seal the lid shut with a few turns, then hand me the "key." The key to my poor dead mother's casket!

"Of course, it's not for *her.* It won't get her into heaven or keep her out. I suppose it has to do with peace of mind."

During the decades of the cold war, peace of mind sold many things: mouthwash, contraceptives, defense budgets.

"To some families *protection* is *very important.*" He would pause. "To others it means *nothing at all.*"

This declarative, according to my tutor, encouraged the customer to consider which kind of family he or she was a part of— one for whom things were *very important* or one for whom things meant *nothing at all.*

"Here, for example"—he'd cross the aisle to a carved-top mahogany—"is a fine hardwood casket, a bit more *dear,* but not a *sealed* casket in the way the metal caskets are. Many families appreciate wooden caskets for their *warmth* and *beauty* and *natural qualities.* Still, the costliest of woods will not last as long as the least expensive metal."

I'd consider the price card on the big mahogany—three times the price of the eighteen-gauge—and say something like "Thanks, but no thanks. Mom would come back to haunt me if I spent that much." Even then, my generation, famously oblivious to "costs," had learned to blame our parents, dead or alive, for any shortage of largesse.

My father, backing through the casket selection from unit to unit, would nod empathetically and move to another metal casket that shone like a new penny.

"This is thirty-two-ounce solid copper, a *permanent* metal. Unlike steel, which might rust or corrode, copper and bronze *oxidize* with age—that green you see on old rooftops, statues, eaves, troughs . . . it gets *stronger and stronger.* These *precious metals* are the best *value* in *protective caskets.*"

I would consider the copper. My father stood his ground. The room was thick with anticipation. *Stronger, precious, values . . . Mom?*

The notions of protection and permanence were organizing principles of my parents' generation. Children of economic collapse and citizens of a planet constantly at war, they were schooled against waste and letting down their guard. Thus, diapers, life insurance, personal-hygiene products, all offered different forms of "protection." There was this general low-grade anxiety over "exposure" and liabilities. Well-engineered tampons, strident regulatory agencies, movie ratings, underarm deodorants, each offered a line of defense against some contagion, embarrassment or invader. That diamonds were forever was some comfort in the face of the ever-present threats to marriage and family. A piece of the rock, a tune from the past that was built to last, seatbelts, Tupperware, sealed caskets and nuclear submarines—to some people these were very important; to others, they meant nothing at all. We were all "right."

When I wouldn't opt for the copper or mahogany or praying hands, my father would eventually stand aside and, with a wave of his arm like a philharmonic conductor, open the rest of the options to me. I'd wander through the showroom, pausing over the carefully worded descriptions and price cards. *Tufted velvet, hand-hammered bronze deposit, $1775.00, solid cherry, stainless steel, cedar, doeskin, 20-gauge nonsealer.* I wanted to see them all, every one, and maybe some catalogs. Were there other colors available? I wondered. I couldn't quite make a decision, it seemed.

In the rosy light of the casket room, at twenty-one, my thoughts would sometimes drift from my choice of caskets to the inventory of my other options. Should I return to school and finish my education? Should I marry Elena Pascuzzi? Should I return to Ireland? Italy? The former Yugoslavia, where I'd met, the month before, a woman who made love in Serbo-Croatian? Should I go into teaching, undertaking, politics or show biz? Nuclear physics or the ministry? Pizza for lunch or Coney Islands? Smoking or non-smoking, cash or charge, acoustic or electric, coffee or tea? Should I get to California on a Harley or on psychedelics? Zen or vegetarian or Christianity?

The abundance of choices made choosing difficult.

"Which one?" My father's voice would yank me from my reveries.

"I don't know." I would tell him. "They're all so lovely."

Thus was I instructed in the sale of caskets. And over the years, I have sold my share to friends and family and perfect strangers. Of course, we don't push protection and permanence anymore. Forever isn't all it was cracked up to be in diamonds or in caskets. Divorce and cremation have taken their toll.

Indeed, the generation in the market now for mortuary wares is redefining death in much the same way that three decades back we redefined sex and gender. I think we thought that we invented , it all.

Disabused of the connection between copulation and conception, we boomers didn't need to be told twice that if we couldn't be with the one we loved (Honey) we ought to love the one we were with. To such tunes, dancing came naturally. Pleasure could be a destination point. Unlike our parents, for whom sex held, quite frequently, bouncing-baby consequences and who, consequently, consigned it to their most intimate and deliberate vocabulary, sex for us was a flexible lexicon. Spontaneous, serendipitous, no strings attached. With some partners, it could be very important. With others, it could mean nothing at all.

Love was "free."

Funerals, I am here to tell you, aren't. And though we are masters at reinvention, and though the fashions of love and grief might change, love and grief remain—the dance and the piper, the tax we pay on our heart's attachments.

If my father sold caskets on protection and permanence, I offer choices, options, New Age alternatives. Where he occupied a world of black and white, ritual and tradition, moral certainty, our rights and wrongs are relative; we roll our own orthodoxies, in Polaroid and Technicolor. His generation buried the dead and burned their garbage; we do landfills and crematoria. He peddled copper and concrete and granite memorials. We do combustible, eco-friendly, video, virtual, cyber-obsequies—"a little something for the ashes?" He sold velvet and satin and crepe interiors. We sell denim and linen and warm-fuzzies.

But these are fashions, always in flux, fickle as the market-place, priced at whatever the traffic will bear. Bookstores are giving shelves formerly filled with *The Joy of Sex* to *The Meaning of Death*. Titles multiply on bereavement and hospice care and "end-of-life issues." TV and talk radio and tabloids follow suit. We boomers in our forties and early fifties are discovering mortality, burying and burning our mothers and fathers, hustling to reinvent the wheels that got our parents and their parents through age and sickness and sadness and loss in case, just in case, it could happen to us. Faced with the deaths of the ones we love, we are stuck between the will to do everything, anything and nothing at all.

And the generation-old arguments over our right to choose are giving way to contentions over our so-called right to die. Aborting and *kevorking* share the same vocabulary—for each there's a coat hanger and a back alley and an old van; bishops and politicos and true believers. The quacks who want to clone us and do us in sound much the same.

Back at the funeral home the hot topics—forgive me—are cremation and designer funerals. My parents' generation, in their seventies now, are buying motor homes and time-shares in casino towns, trading in their piece of the rock for a piece of the action, taking a walk on the wild side of slot machines and casual sex, beginning to behave like their children used to: scattered, mobile, portable, still crazy after all these years. They do not want to be a burden to their children. They do not want to be "grounded" to the graves they bought, pre-need, back in the old days when people stayed put. Their ashes are FedExed and parcel-posted and UPSed around the hemisphere day and night in little packages, roughly the weight of a bowling ball, roughly the shape of that first starter home, roughly the size of a coffee can squared. Not nearly the full, life-sized burden of a casket, not nearly the bother or expense. Less for them is less. For us it's more. They get sent back from Vegas and Phoenix, Florida and the Carolinas, to old homes in the cold North and Rust Belt states.

Still, their sons and daughters, in receipt of these tiny reminders, are beginning to wonder, *Is that all there is?* Is it enough to get out our cell phones and our gold cards and have our dead elders disappeared with no more pause than it takes to order up sushi to go? Can we distance ourselves entirely from the physical realities of death and still expect to enjoy the physical wonders of life?

If the old become young again, maybe the young are coming of age.

Always the demographic bullies on the block, now that we boomers are grieving and dying, grief and death are all the rage. The market is bullish on ritual and metaphor, for acting out our hurts the way our ancients did. Whether we burn or bury our dead or blast them into space is less important than what we do before we dispose of them. More and more we care for our own dying. More and more we are making up new liturgies to say good-bye. More and more we seem willing to engage fully in the process of leave-taking. We rise early to watch the TV obsequies of princesses and modern saints. We read the obits every day. We eulogize, elegize and memorialize with vigor. The trade is brisk in wakes and funerals. We sell copper and combustibles, bronze and biodegradables, eco-friendly and economy models. We do urns that look like golf bags and go to cemeteries with names like golf courses. You can buy a casket off the Internet, or buy plans for a self-built coffin table or one that doubles as a bookshelf or an armoire until you "need" it. There's a kind of push for "do-it-yourself" funerals, as if grief were ever anything but. Cremated remains can be cast into bookends or paper weights or duck decoys. They can be recycled as memorial kitty litter, sprinkled on our rose bushes, mixed with our oil paints to add texture to fresh masterpieces. We have, as Batesville Casket Company calls its latest marketing approach, "Options." And as the demographic aneurysm gets nearer to bursting in two or three decades, the marketplace is readying for another boom. Soon every off-ramp on every interstate across the continent will have a Best Buy, Builders Square, Burger King, Barnes & Noble and Casket Express. The expanding choices in mortuary wares make it seem as if we really have choices about mortality.

The facts of life and death remain the same. We live and die, we love and grieve, we breed and disappear. And between these existential gravities, we search for meaning, save our memories, leave a record for those who will remember us.

I remember my father. I remember being his son. I hear my father's caution in the way I caution my son now—and his sister and his brothers—about life's changes and dangers, about drugs and drink and being "sexually active." We talk about making responsible choices, safe sex, committed relationships, condoms and consequences: permanence and protection come round again.

One of these days I'll have to teach them caskets.

The Way We Are

I hope my pony knows the way back home.
—TOM WAITS

"I want to remember him the way he was."

I GET TOLD THIS A LOT by the ones who love the ones who die. Most times there is a casket involved.

"THIS IS GOING TO BE A CLOSED CASKET," they tell me, in the voice we are trained to discuss our options in. Like sunroofs or modems. It's easier to talk about things than people.

"HE WOULDN'T WANT PEOPLE SEEING HIM like this." As if the dead, safe in whatever heaven or oblivion they inhabit, give a rap about appearances. Maybe he got skinny with AIDS or prostate cancer, or went green with liver failure, or bulbous with renal failure, or flipped his semi on the interstate. Maybe he hanged himself from a basement rafter or drove his snowmobile into the side of a tree, or curled up fetal in the end, a shadow only of his former self.

"IT'S NOT HIM ANYMORE," they say emphatically.
Or "her." These things happen to "hers" as well—the cancers and the cardiac arrests, the lapses of caution that do us in.

"I want to remember him the way he was."

And who could blame them? Who'd want to see someone they love like this? Whatever way they got like this. Dead.

"But remembering him the way he was," I say, slowly, deliberately, as if the listener were breakable, "begins by dealing with the way he is." I'm an apostle of the present tense. After years and years of directing funerals, I've come to the conclusion that seeing is the hardest and most helpful part. The truth, even when it hurts, has a healing in it, better than fiction or fantasy. When someone dies, it is not them we fear seeing, it is them *dead*. It is the death. We fear that seeing will be believing.

We fear not seeing too. We search the wreckage and the ruins, the battle fields and ocean floors. We must find our dead to let the loss be real.

Confrontation, closure, catharsis, denial—these are words I learned in mortuary school. And for going on thirty years, I've stood with bereaved parents, the widowed and heartsore, in front of open caskets and over open graves. And I've waited with the families of abducted children, tornado victims, foreign missionaries, drowned toddlers, Peace Corps volunteers, Vietnam and Gulf War casualties—waited for their precious dead to be found and named and sent back home to them to be buried or burned, mourned and remembered. I've listened while well-meaning but ill-informed clergy, nervous in-laws, neighbors and old friends sought to comfort the living by telling them the body in the box was "just a shell." The operative word in this is *just*. The effort to minimize the hurt by minimizing the loss, pretending that a dead body has lost its meaning or identity, is another tune we whistle past the graveyard. The sad truths I've been taught by the families of the dead are these: seeing is believing; knowing is better than not knowing; to name the hurt returns a kind of comfort; the grief ignored will never go away. For those whose sons and daughters, husbands, wives, mothers, fathers and friends went off alive and never did return, the worst that can happen has already happened. The light and air of what is known, however difficult, is better than the dark. The facts of death, like the facts of life, are required learning.

But oh, so difficult, the tuition.

I want to remember my son the way he was.

He wouldn't want people seeing him like this.

It's not him anymore.

I want to remember him the way he was—that bright and beaming boy with the blue eyes and the freckles in the photos, holding the walleye on his grandfather's dock, or dressed in his first suit for his sister's grade-school graduation, or sucking his thumb while drawing at the kitchen counter, or playing his first guitar, or posing with the brothers from down the block on his first day of school. I want to remember him in chest waders in the river with his brothers and me, or up at the cottage, those summers of his boyhood, a hero to his younger cousins, the pied piper with plenty of time, or with his stepmother on the roller coaster at Cedar Point, or there—there on the beach beside me before the divorce, it was July in that picture of the two of us his mother took—me on my elbows, him on his knees, me in my thirties, him at three and I'm showing him something in my hand—I can't for the life of me remember—and his mother must have just called his name or said "Smile" because he's smiling, the blue of the sea and the day behind us, that moment there, when everything was well. I have videos too—of talent shows and First Communion, soccer match-es and skateboarding in the parking lot next door, or playing drums. God, he was really good on the drums. And the guitar—really anything with strings. I've some of him on tape—his first songs, his first recordings. I have his first paintings, his first note-books full of still lifes, figures, portraits, body studies. He has such talents. I want to remember him the way he was.

I want to remember him the way he was, with one grand-mother's red hair and the other's eye for shape and color, with his mother's smile and my curiosities, before that first sip, whenever it was, first quickened in him the unquenchable thirst; when his body's chemistry locked and loaded on what it was it had been waiting for all these years, this little bit of giddy oblivion, this alco-hol, this sedation.

He wouldn't want people seeing him like this—laid out, cold, pale, dead to the world, a corpse that has forgotten to hold its breath—smelling like so many corpses I've smelled for whom the issue of whether or not they had a drinking problem has become moot. Once they make it to the bright lights, porcelain table, uni-versal precautions stage, when their bagged viscera smell like stale excess and their cranium is wadded with cotton and stitched shut by the morgue, once they make it to my embalming room, whether they are a dead social drinker or a dead alcoholic makes little dif-ference. They are dead.

So if, thanks to guardian angels or maybe his sainted grand-mothers' interventions, he's not dead yet, all the same, he wouldn't want people seeing him like this—dead drunk, passed out, half in and half out of his clothes—horizontal on the leather couch, some-place between seizure and coma, dying by doses, dead to the world.

It's not him anymore. It hasn't been for some time now. Not since he was fourteen and the thirst became a sickness. It is the thirst and sickness that has dogged my people in every generation that I remember.

My grandfathers were vaguely bingey men who'd learned to consummate big deals with drink—the wakes and weddings and baptisms, hunting and fishing trips, Fourths of July, Christmases and family crises. My mother's father died young, of a big heart, huffing and puffing to his purple end, before we formed many memories of him. My father's father, when my father went to war, swore off the drink in a deal he made with God for his only son's safe return. And when the young marine came home, my grandfather kept his end of the bargain. I remember going with him to the bars up and down Six Mile Road. "Bumming," he called it—hanging out with his pals, talking local sports and politics, showing off his grandsons—but he'd drink only Vernors ginger ale, and died sober and happy that his son had outlived him.

But World War II and the First Marines taught my father more than fear and killing. They taught him fearlessness and drinking. He came home skinny and malarial, as in the snapshots, our mother's name tattooed on his arm, enrolled in mortuary school, married his sweetheart, moved to the suburbs and began making babies and a future for us. I remember the cases of Stroh's beer on the basement landing, how he and his pals would play cards some nights, or sit out on the porch on a Sunday listening to ball games. They would talk and drink and laugh and be happy.

I don't know when my father's drinking turned on him, when his thirst turned to sickness. I don't know. I saw him drunk only once.

I was sixteen. His father had died eight weeks before of a sudden heart attack. Now it was New Year's. My mother couldn't get him out of the car. He claimed he was having a heart attack. The doctor came and called it "sympathetic pains." My mother wasn't buying "sympathy." Whatever it was for my dad, for my mother that night was enough. She wouldn't cover for him anymore. She wouldn't pretend for him anymore. She wouldn't keep his dinners warm or secrets anymore. It was her threat, if his drinking continued, to send his sons out looking for him, up and down his haunts on Woodward Avenue, that got him to swear off. And swear is what he did. God damn it. He could do it. He would show her. He would show us all. A year or so later, when he missed my youngest brother's birthday party, getting too blurry over a boozy lunch with a casket salesman to get home for the cake and ice cream, the remorse and guilt were more than he could bear.

That night he went to his first AA meeting. I was not quite eighteen, working at the funeral home, when my father told me he was an alcoholic. He could not promise he'd never drink again. But he said he hoped to be sober that day. He asked me to pray for him.

Twenty-five years later we buried him with a bottle of whiskey under each elbow, in case, as he sometimes speculated, maybe in heaven he could drink again. His quarter century's sobriety was a gift.

If most of his sons and daughters inherited his disease, most likewise followed in his sobriety. Whether blind luck or the grace of God kept us from killing ourselves or someone else, hard as we tried to, is hard to say. Either way, we all outlived our father and our mother and found ourselves having to make our own peace with drink and drugs and their afflictions. Whether we were problem drinkers or not, whenever there were problems, we were drinking.

For me it happened after years of successfully ducking punches and dodging disasters. I never liked the beer they were drinking in high school, but learned in college to like whiskey. Marijuana mostly put me to sleep, and I mistrusted the way it turned ignoramuses into philosophers. I tried some uppers when I worked at the state hospital, which made me jumpy, and I got sick on wine, and vodka seemed medicinal, but whiskey was lovely and the drinking of it made me feel mannish and Irish and worthy and numb.

By twenty I'd gotten into fights, fallen off of buildings, driven into ditches, lost my way—mayhems within the "normal," "acceptable" range of youthful dereliction. After I married and the family came along, I became more cautious. With more to lose, I learned how to manage my drinking. I stayed close to home, mostly drinking with poet friends and Rotarians—genius and business providing good cover. I'd get a little tight on Tuesday nights from cocktails at Harold Hansen's house, followed by dinner with the Rotary, followed by afterglow at the local drinkery. About the time I could not feel my jaw, it would be time to drive home, less than a mile, and since the police chief was a fellow Rotarian, his deputies might follow me home for safety's sake, but unless I ran into or over something I was left alone. Weekends I'd binge a little with neighbors and friends, at dinner parties and barbecues, card games now and then. There were a few "episodes," but nothing to panic over. I made only the usual fool of myself. I was your garden-variety suburban boozer, and for the most part it made me happier than sadder. I might look a little stupid, blather on too much, get a little sloppy, but I didn't scream or get into fights or ignore my duties, so what harm? I was functioning. I might've gone on like that forever.

This sickness, this thirst, this alcoholism, I've come to think of as a card that comes in everyone's deck—a joker, maybe—but it is there for sure. When it is going to turn up is anyone's guess. For most, I suppose, they never get to it. It's down at the bottom where it is supposed to be. They don't outlive their possible draws. For some the deck is shuffled differently, maybe by genetics or the luck of the Irish or the star-crossed heavens, who's to know? But they get to the joker that much quicker. It turns up when they're forty-ish, fiftyish, sixty or more. Others find it earlier, or it finds them. The more they drink the less good it does them, but the joker keeps winking at them as if everything is fine.

It was after I divorced that it began to turn for me. It was, mind you, a divorce made in heaven. She deserved better. So did I. We agreed on almost nothing—money, religion, the rearing of children. We made beautiful babies and enjoyed doing it, but otherwise we were at odds. I never really much admired her. I could live with her, but I could live without her too. It seems she thought as much of me. When it was over I was left with physical custody of our toddler and preteens, half my estimated life expectancy, a double mortgage on the house, and this low-grade, ever-ready anger at anything that moved. And there was this fear, like a knot always tightening inside me that could be loosened a little by nightly doses of alcohol. The blather began to turn bitter, the foolishness turned calculating, I seethed. My children were caught between my fears for what might happen to them and my anger at what had happened to me. They were damned if they did and if they didn't.

I ruled by guilt and shame and sarcasm. My ever-shifting mood kept them on their toes, always trying to curry favor with me. It was easier than reason or listening to them. I don't know how long we lived like this. Whether it was weeks or months or years—I just don't know. And I don't know if the divorce was coincidental with my drinking going bad, or correlated to it, or the thing that caused it. Like a tumor or infection, it is hard to say when or why drink gets malignant, when the thirst gets terminal. But once it does it no longer matters—what happens or what doesn't happen. I drank because that's what sick drinkers do, whether to celebrate the good day or compensate for the bad one, whether shit happens or doesn't happen. Because it is Friday is reason enough. Because it's November will also do.

But I remember, and pray I always remember, the morning in April, it was a Monday, making bologna sandwiches for the bag lunches and shouting orders to the older boys and their sister about their homework and their school uniforms and how they'd better hurry or we'd be late and I was harried with house duties and hung over from a bottle of Bushmills that I had finished the night before to celebrate nothing in particular and I had to drive them to school and get back and shower and shave and get dressed for a ten o'clock funeral because I was the guy whose name was on the sign and if I didn't do it it wouldn't be done right and here it was Monday and I was already playing catch-up-ball with the office and the carpool and the cash flow and the kids and I'm slamming the apples and cookies in with the bologna sandwiches and cursing my fates and barking out orders and wondering what a guy has to do for a drink around here when I see my darling boy who is nine in this memory sitting at the counter with his bowl of Froot Loops and orange juice in his blue shirt and the look in his eyes as he's looking at me is fear, godhelpus, and he is afraid of me, of my anger and of my fear.

I didn't know if I was an alcoholic. But I knew that I never wanted to see that fear of me again in the eyes of any of my children. So I didn't drink that night, and the next morning, all other things being equal, I was not as angry. And the morning after that was calmer still. And whether or not I was an alcoholic, the removal of alcohol made things some better.

For months I stayed dry for the sake of my children and was feeling like "what a guy," and no wonder the court-appointed shrinks found me the more "stable" parent and the judge had "awarded" me custody, what with my willpower and moral courage and the rest. I was feeling pretty special, kind of like a sacrificial lamb, or local hero, or martyr for the cause; kind of like a guy who gave up his one wee consolation for the kids, kind of like I imagined moms must feel like most of the time.

That October I was traveling through southern California, giving poetry readings at schools and libraries, afraid that I hadn't written a line in months, afraid that my children were three thousand miles back home with my woman friend, afraid that none of my poems would last fifty years, afraid that my mother was dying of lung cancer, afraid of what would happen if I bought a bottle and took the day off, afraid of what would happen if I didn't.

Instead of taking a walk on the beach or writing the great American poem, or staring into the Pacific, I spent the whole day holed up pacing and vexed, wondering about a drink. Not drinking was taking up as much time and energy as drinking would have taken. There had to be an easier way. I found the number in the phone book on the first page of A's. I called and told them where I was. They told me where to go. That's how I got to my first AA meeting—at a church called All Saints on a beach in Santa Bar-

bara. The first time I said that I was an alcoholic, I wasn't really sure. And when I said it—"My name's Tom and I'm an alcoholic"—it felt like diving into cold water on a hot day. Still, the sky didn't fall, the earth didn't quake, the folks at the table responded as if I'd told them Wednesday follows Tuesday or the Yankees play ball. Later, when I told the people I really loved that I thought possibly there was this off chance, one in a million really, that I might be alcoholic, "Oh, really?" they said. "Do tell! What was your first clue?" Neither perfect strangers nor my nearest and dearest were very startled by this intelligence. It seems I was the very last to know.

In time I went from dry to sober. In time it seemed less like giving up something and more like getting something out of the blue. In time the fear gave way to faith, the anger to a kind of gratitude. The shit that still happened did not overwhelm. I didn't have to drink about it.

The conventional wisdom among recovering drunks is that the sickness leaves us three possibilities, like that old game show *Let's Make a Deal*. We get well. We go crazy. Or we die. I keep wishing there was another choice, say, behind Door Number Four, where we can all have a drink and talk it over. But it seems that there are only three. We stop drinking and get sober. Or we keep drinking and spend a lot of time in jail or hospitals or asylums or on the street. Or we keep drinking and spend a lot of time in the cemetery.

Nor is there a cure. We can't be fixed by any surgery or pill that will let us drink or drug like ordinary humans. Even when we are getting better, the disease is getting worse. We can get a life-long remission, but once the drinking turns ugly there is no return. A pickle can't become a cucumber again.

And I hate that part sometimes—the way they've got these tidy little bromides like that one just now, about the pickle. There's one for every possible contingency. "Fake it till you make it" someone will say, or "One day at a time," or "Stay out of using places and using faces." Give me a break. Here I am a goddamn published poet who has been ignored in several countries in the Western world and translated into Serbo-Croatian and left out of several of the best anthologies and I've got to listen to rhymes like these? "Walk the walk and talk the talk." "The past is history, the future's a mystery." Or some quirky little alliterative like "Let Go Let God." As if we ever let go of anything without leaving claw marks in it. And God? This Higher Power business? Why can't they just settle on a name like any other bunch? Yahweh or Jehovah or Jesus or Steve? And what about these little acronyms, like KISS (Keep It Simple Stupid), or don't get HALT (Hungry Angry Lonely or Tired)! How is a guy who's always been TBBTO (The Brains Behind the Operation) supposed to take such things seriously? Because even when they tell me it's a simple program for complex people, I think there must be more to it than that; more to it than some old-timer grinning at a table and holding up his thumb, saying "Don't take a drink," and then, on his index finger, "Go to meetings." Just two things? That's it? Give me a break. What's a guy who's read Dante and Pushkin need with meetings and head cases, and what does it mean when these nuts begin to make sense to him? And why can't it be like riding a bike—once you've got it you won't ever forget it? Though I've quit drinking like a drunk, I'm still inclined to thinking like one. Hear that little rhyme in there? And there's always this blathering idiot in my ear saying I can toss a few back like any normal guy, like eight out of ten of my fellow citizens, for whom enough is enough. What harm would it do? And the only thing between me and believing that voice and following its instructions are the men and women I meet with regularly who help me to remember the way I was.

Which, godhelpus, maybe is the way my son is now—frightened and angry, stuck between egomania and inferiority complex, sick and tired, dead drunk. If his thirst is like mine he won't be able to talk his way out of it, think his way out of it, read or write or run his way out of it, lie or cheat or buy his way out of it. The only victory is in an admission of defeat. The only weapon is surrender.

Still, the father in me—the take-charge, I'll handle it, you can count on me, master of our destiny fellow—wants to fix it for him. Protecting and providing, that's what dads do. I've always been pretty good at scripts and I've got one for him with a happy ending if only he'll just learn the lines by heart and do exactly what I tell him to do.

Years back—it was the autumn of his freshman year in high school—when his grades went to hell and his smile disappeared and the music in our house got dark, I took him out of school one morning and said I was taking him to find out what the matter was. I said I thought there must be something very wrong to account for all the changes I could see. Maybe a tumor or a loose screw or maybe, because it ran in our family, drink and drugs and addictions. I told him we wouldn't quit until we found out what accounted for the darkness that had descended on his life and times. No diagnostic stone would be unturned.

So we started with the drug and alcohol assessment, which turned up, unremarkably, positive. He was fourteen and trying anything that came his way. So I explained how it was like diabetes or an allergy and he should know that he was in danger because of his family history. A beer for him, a joint, whatever pills or powders were going round, might do more damage than "experimenting"— which is what we parents tell ourselves our sons and daughters are always doing.

By midwinter things had gone from bad to worse. I tried my best to ignore the obvious—his lackluster grades, the long hours in his room, the distance he began to keep, the smell of alcohol that was always on him. One night he came home besotted and muddy. He had passed out in the park, in a puddle. How he kept from drowning, how he crawled home, remains a mystery. The next morning I took him to a treatment center that one of my brothers had been to before. They took him in for thirteen days, detoxed him, told him that he was alcoholic, and told us he should get long-term care, that his alcoholism was chronic, acute and full-blown. There would be no cure, but with treatment he might get into a pattern of recovery that would allow him to live without using in a using world. We all wept. Inquiries were made. An adolescent treatment center was found. It was at a hospital on the south side of Cleveland and was named for a saint I'd never heard of before. My son said if I made him go he'd kill himself. There was a calm in his voice that said he wasn't bluffing. I said he was killing himself already. I said I'd buried lots of boys for lots of fathers. I said if I was going to have to be like those poor hollow men, standing in the funeral home with my darling son in a casket, while neighbors and friends and family gathered to say they wished there was something they could say or do, I told him, if he was going to be dead either way, at least he wouldn't die of my denial, my ignorance, my unwillingness to deal with the way we are. I said if he killed himself I would miss him terribly, I would never forget him and always love him and I'd hate to outlive him but I'd survive. And I'd call someone before I'd drink about it.

Calling this bet broke something inside.

Every Friday for three months I'd drive down and get him, bring him home for two nights and take him back Sunday in the afternoon. The turkey vultures and red-tailed hawks hovering over the Ohio Turnpike are all I remember of those travels now. It was a summer lost to our disease. Everywhere I looked was the shadow of death. But he survived it and came home and got a sponsor and started going to AA meetings and the darkness seemed to lift from him. His grades were good, his music improved, he was painting, writing, smiling again. He started dating. For all of a year he went on like this and I got to thinking it had all been worth it, the driving and the money and all the madness, because he was fixed, better, thriving again. He was living the life he was supposed to live. So when the old signs started up again I didn't see them. I didn't want to see them. I'd quit looking. I kept wanting to see him according to the script I'd written in which all these demons were behind him, before he had anything more to lose.

It was halfway through his third year of high school when I told him I couldn't ignore the obvious anymore. I couldn't live with a using alcoholic. It was making me crazy, all the pretense and worry. I asked him to go back into treatment, or take up an outpatient program, or return to his AA meetings, anything besides relapsing again. He refused. I told him I couldn't live with him. He called his mother. She came and got him.

In the best of all cases, he would have had to move to her side of the state, lose his drinking buddies, find a new school and new buyers and suppliers, pay the price for his drinking on demand. Instead, his mother got him an apartment here in town so he could stay in the same school, hang out at the old haunts and have fewer of the parental hoops to jump through.

It is nearly impossible for any divorced parent to bypass the opportunity to save a child from the other parent. Rescue is what parents are good at. And if a son or daughter needs rescuing from the same asshole that you couldn't live with, well, who's to blame them? Of course, the children pay dearly for such second opinions, in discipline avoided, diluted rules, old wars and old divisions redeclared. By the time most parents have evolved beyond such temptations, their children are married and parents on their own.

One night in midwinter I found him passed out in a snowbank on Main Street. He was drunk, frozen, full of remorse, mumbling things like "You shouldn't have to see me like this." I called his mother and said she could come and get him. She took him to the hospital because we didn't know what he might have taken. Or if he had frostbite. Or if his shivering was a seizure. When the emergency room pronounced him out of danger, she called the number my wife had given her. It was another treatment center. She buckled on her courage and took him there.

He spent twelve days in that drunk tank. He came out and returned more or less immediately to his relapse, only this time he tried to "manage" it better. His mother, wanting to be helpful, hopeful, trusting, because she loves him, signed for his driver's license and bought him a car. He got picked up for stealing wine from the grocer's, busted for possession of beer in the park, lost one job and then another, dented the car in a parking lot. Otherwise we saw little of him. The high school gave him a diploma. He lost his driver's license and got a year's probation.

On the strength of his portfolio he got admitted to a posh art school, and because I wanted badly to believe, because I wanted badly to say, in spite of everything I knew to the contrary, maybe talent and promise and art could overcome disease, maybe he had outgrown it, I paid his tuition, room and board, and watched and waited and said my prayers. One weekend he got picked up for driving drunk without a valid license and spent the night in jail. His grades at first were not great and then they disappeared. He spent another weekend in jail for his crimes and got another year's probation.

When he asked to move home this summer from the dormitory at the art school I said I would not live with a using drunk. He said he understood. That's the way we talk. I couldn't say I wouldn't live with him. He couldn't say he wouldn't drink again.

In the space between what we didn't say, my stupid hope and his sickness flourished. I wanted to remember him the way he was. And wanting it so bad, I welcomed him, half-hoping some of the lost months of his lost years would return. But they are gone and the summer has gone from bad to worse. He's tried so hard to keep from being a bother. He tries to come home after we've gone to bed. Some nights he calls and says he's staying with friends and some nights he falls asleep on the couch downstairs. He holds his breath and kisses us. He says he loves us. He really doesn't want me to worry. He doesn't want to bother me with his drinking. He doesn't want to disturb my remembrances and I want to remember the way he was and I know he wouldn't want people seeing him like this because really that's not him anymore, there on the couch, at four-thirty in the early morning, neither sleeping nor dead but somewhere in between with no clear indication of which way he's going.

Putting him out of my house is like sending a child to chemotherapy. It hurts so bad to think I cannot save him, protect him, keep him out of harm's way, shield him from pain. What good are fathers if not for these things? Why can't he be a boy again, safe from these perils and disasters? Lately I'm always on the brink of breaking. But remembering the way he was begins by dealing with the way he is, which is sick, sick to death, with something that tells him he's "not so bad"—that jail and joblessness and loneliness and blackouts are all within the "normal" range. His thirst puts him utterly beyond my protection but never outside the loop of my love. If he is going to die on a couch some night, of alcohol poisoning or from choking on his own puke, or burned up from a cigarette he passed out smoking; or if he drives his car into a bridge abutment or over some edge from which there is no return; or if he gets so crazy with pain and fear he puts a pistol in his mouth, Oh my God, the best I can manage is not my couch, not my car, not my pistol, Oh my God. If I cannot save him, I will not help him die, or welcome his killer in my home.

What I've learned from my sobriety, from the men and women who keep me sober, is how to pray. Blind drunks who get sober get a kind of blind faith—not so much a vision of who God is, but who God isn't, namely me.

When I was a child all of my prayers sounded like "Gimme, Gimme." I wanted a Jerry Mahoney puppet, to fly like Superman, and for my brothers and sisters to be adopted by other kindly parents and leave me and my mother and father alone. I got none of these things. These prayers were never answered.

When I was my son's age, I'd always begin with "Show me, Lord." I wanted a sign. I wanted God to prove Himself or Herself or Itself to me. In this I was a typical youth, full of outrage and arrogance and bravado. Nothing ever happened. I never saw a statue move or lightning strike or heard any voices that I couldn't account for. The ones I prayed to be blighted thrived. The proofs I prayed for never appeared. None of these prayers were ever answered.

For years, twenty of them anyway, as a new husband, new parent, new funeral director in town, as a social drinker and a working poet, I'd pray, albeit infrequently, "Why me, God?" The more I drank, the more I prayed it. Why do I have to work harder, longer, for less thanks or wages? Why does that magazine publish only brunettes or professors or free verse or the famous? Why can't I sleep in or get a break or win the lotto? Why would any woman leave a man like me? And when my inventory of "why me's" was exhausted, I would ask on behalf of my fellow man. Why did cars crash, planes fall out of the sky, bad things happen to good people? Why, if Anyone's in charge, did children die? Or folks go homeless? Or others get away with murder? I was carping daily, a victim of my all too often self-inflicted wounds. The silence out of heaven to these questions was real. Why wasn't God listening? I wanted to know. And before I'd agree to step one foot in heaven, I had a list of things I wanted explanations for.

There's a reason we are given two ears and one mouth.

Someone told me that I should just say "Thanks," and that all my prayers should begin that way and never stray far from the notion that life was a gift to be grateful for. I began by giving thanks for my family, for the blessings to my household, the gifts of my children. Then the daylight and the nightfall and the weather. Then the kindness you could see in humankind, their foibles and their tender mercies. I could even be grateful for the ex-wife, the tax man, the gobshites who run the world and ruin everything. The more I mouthed my thanks for them, the less they bothered me. There's another thing to be thankful for. I could be thankful even for this awful illness—cunning, baffling and powerful—that has taught me to weep and laugh out loud and better and for real. And thankful that, of all the fatal diseases my son might have gotten, he got one for which there is this little sliver of a hope that if he surrenders, he'll survive. Whatever happens, God will take care of him.

And every time I say it, the prayer gets answered. Someone, out of the blue, every day—maybe my wife or someone at the office or the guy in the line at the airport or something in a letter that came in the mail, or something in the lives of my sons or daughter—someone gives out with a sign or wonder in the voice of God, in some other voice than mine, to answer my prayer. Every day, every time, never fails, if I just say "Thanks," I'll get the answer, before the darkness comes—"You're welcome," it says. "You're welcome."

Notes on "A Note on the Rapture to His True Love"

Among the few consolations of what has been called writer's block is the assurance that, so long as one has it, one is, indeed, a writer. Of course, the longer it goes the more it resembles, and risks being mistaken for, proctologist's block, real estate agent's block, and other *obstructions ordinaire*.

For this reason, years ago, I devised a formula by which relief from such affliction is nearly guaranteed.

The formula is simple. You may try it at home.

First you sit down—a sensible protocol whatever the blockage—and consider an inanimate object in your house. This will keep you from writing about pets and children too much.

Next, look out of doors, beyond, if you please, the domestic interior. Let your gaze fall on something out there in the landscape or geography.

Third, pull something from the daily papers—an article or obit or something from the want ads. Display ads from political-action committees or labor unions, while not entirely forbidden, are known to produce poor results.

And fourth, take something from the TV.

Now endeavor to relate these seemingly unrelated apparitions in verse—for isn't this the enterprise of poetry? To appre-
hend the kinship in the distant cousins of happenstance and image
and utterance? Or vice versa? Lest any quibble should arise, assign
yourself some formal tasking in advance: a rhyme scheme or a
verse form—a pantoum or sestina, say, or a metrical or acoustic
hoop through which you agree, in advance, to jump.

Truth told, this multimedia approach results in remarkable
disappointments—poems of such abundant mediocrity that I burn
them or affix to them the names of poets I dislike and post them to
The New Yorker. At least one—which I shall not name here—was
accepted for publication and appeared in a summer double issue,
the generous check and the week-long fame assigned to the
account of a fellow I meant to damage. He later made it the title
poem for his sixth collection, claiming in the eventual interview
that it had come to him in a dream.

Such was not the case with "A Note on the Rapture to His
True Love." It was, to use the conventional bromide, a work of perspiration not inspiration. It was ever and only mine—the first
deliberate poetic effort that bore fruit sufficient to please me after
months of silence.

In this poem, a blue ceramic salad bowl (the gift of a neighbor who'd had an unsuccessful garage sale) combined with the
same neighbor's sugar maple tree, to which I added (from the
Detroit Free Press of that day) the news of the discovery, quite by
accident, of a new prime number—an item of interest to more
people than we can know—a number with two hundred thousand
digits, divisible (like 11 and 13 and 1,009) only by 1 and by itself.

Such numbers cannot be manufactured. This one required a massive computer's efforts for days and days. And the article went on to articulate the hope that by doing a sort of mathematical postmortem on the new number, a formula for the generation of more might be found. Why this is important is anyone's guess. As for the TV—we'd only just lately gotten cable in Milford, and I was up nights channel-surfing between infomercials and religious broadcasting, especially Jim and Tammy Bakker, Before the Fall, we might say. I never sent money or touched the TV screen for a healing, but to say I was transfixed by the sermons would be an understatement. A word Jim Bakker used over and over was a word I loved but did not understand. *Rapture*, as the concept by which (either pre-Tribulations or post-Tribulations) the saved among us would disappear, assumed into heaven like the BVM, had never been explained to Catholic children until it was too late to be appreciated. No doubt Jewish children are kept similarly in the dark. The idea that you might be sitting in some five-star eatery, sharing a *crème brûlée* and other intimacies with a woman friend only to have her vanish in the moment and twinkling, leaving only the spoon and the bill to be paid, filled me with a sense of the Glory of God. I loved the word. Especially the verb form. And I yearned to use it in a poem. I tried to get it into this one, but I couldn't. So I put it in the title.

As for the formal imperative—it was getting late. I hadn't written a line yet, so busy had I been at the invention of this formula. Simplicity, I reckoned, ought be the rule. A simple rhyme scheme, to make it memorable and acoustically stimulating. In my poem, accordingly (the full text of which is about to follow), it might be noticed that *room* rhymes quite nicely with *room* and *soon* with *soon* and *turn* with *turn*. This will happen a hundred out of every one hundred tries. You can try this part at home as well.

Late in the effort it occurred to me that I might write only one hundred or two hundred poems in my lifetime, unlike the greats, who write them every day. This is when I angled it (deftly, some reviewers have said) toward the mention of my dear wife, who had for her part left me pretty much alone, not wanting, I suppose, to distract the creative frenzy. Among the highest and best uses of poetry, third only perhaps to the poxing of our enemies and the commemoration of the dead, is the wooing, outright, of our darlings.

A NOTE ON THE RAPTURE
TO HIS TRUE LOVE

A blue bowl on the table in the dining room
fills with sunlight. From a sunlit room
I watch my neighbor's sugar maple turn
to shades of gold. It's late September. Soon . . .
Soon as I'm able I intend to turn
to gold myself. Somewhere I've read that soon
they'll have a formula for prime numbers
and once they do, the world's supposed to end
the way my neighbor always said it would—
in fire. I'll bet we'll all be given numbers
divisible by One and by themselves
and told to stand in line the way you would
for prime cuts at the butcher's. In the end,
maybe it's every man for himself.
Maybe it's someone hollering All Hands On
Deck! Abandon Ship! Women and Children First!
Anyway, I'd like to get my hands on

you. I'd like to kiss your eyelids and make love
as if it were our last time, or the first,
or else the one and only form of love
divisible by which I yet remain myself.
Mary, folks are disappearing one by one.
They turn to gold and vanish like the leaves
of sugar maples. But we can save ourselves.
We'll pick our own salvations, one by one,
from a blue bowl full of sunlight until none is left.

Decca, Dinky,
Benji & Me

J essica Mitford changed my life.
I was fifteen, working nights
and weekends at my father's
funeral home greeting mourners at the door and moving flowers
and caskets, when *The American Way of Death* first appeared. My
father bought it and said I should read it.

So much has changed since that summer of 1963. Kennedy,
Vietnam, color TV, free love and frequent flyer miles. How we live
and die has changed but *that* we do remains. And so much of what
we do when someone dies has been shaped by Ms. Mitford's classic exposé—most surely in America where, having ignored his cau-
tions, I went about my father's business. I've been doing funerals
for going on thirty years.

Most every family with whom I've dealt has brought a version
of Ms. Mitford's book with them. Whether or not they ever read it,
her caricature of our family's business entered the conventional
wisdom and the common parlance undisturbed. To an enterprise
shrouded in darkness she brought the bright light of her curiosity,
her wry humor and her wary indignation, and it has never been the
same since her.

It was over dinner in the East Village last summer that I was discussing these changes with Decca's (as Jessica Mitford was known since childhood) daughter, Constancia Romilly (whom Decca nicknamed Dinky), and with Benjamin (Benji) Treuhaft, Dinky's half-brother and Decca's youngest son. I had questions about their mother's forthcoming book, *The American Way of Death Revisited,* and about her life and times and death in the summer of 1996, quite sudden, as it turned out, from lung cancer.

"You should have seen my mother's funeral," Benjamin said. "Everybody loved it! They really really really liked it because there was no gloom."

I asked if they thought their mother would have approved, what with her famous preferences for simplicity and cost controls. Her body had been cremated, the ashes scattered in the Pacific, but after that things got, well, elaborate.

"The person who dies doesn't get to say anything about their funeral," Dinky said. "No matter how many books they might have written about it. The funeral is for the people who are left behind. They get to do whatever they want. No matter what the person wanted. So I used to tell Decca, we're going to do whatever we want . . . we're going to have a New Orleans band."

Dinky Romilly is like her mother. She is lovely and endearing. She has her mother's eyes, her mother's smile—or the commingled grins of Decca and Esmond, the young exiles beaming from behind the Roma Bar in Miami nearly sixty years ago, before Dinky or Benji or me, in a photo from the first volume of Decca's autobiography *Hons & Rebels.* In a snapshot I have of Dinky at Bellevue Hospital, where she directs a nursing program in palliative care, there are the same fine features, broad eyebrows, tiny shoulders, bright smile, the sense of a genepool repeating itself.

Born in the Cotswolds in 1917, the daughter of rather fascist aristocrats, and sibling to a pair of now deceased Nazi sisters, Jessica Mitford rebelled by becoming what another sister (neither fascist nor Nazi), the novelist Nancy Mitford, called "a ballroom communist"—someone who can endure both the free clinic with the other needy mothers and the island in the Hebrides she inherits; the type who tips well but likes to shoplift. You know, an enigma.

Newly wed to her cousin Esmond Romilly, a nephew of Churchill's, she ran off, in 1937, to fight the forces of evil in Spain. Her father disowned her. After their first daughter, Julia, died of measles, they moved to America. Esmond was killed in action during World War II, leaving her with another infant daughter, Constancia, and a government job in Washington D.C. with the Office of Price Administration—"as close to the frontline of the war against Fascism as anything in Washington," she wrote in her second autobiography, *A Fine Old Conflict.* "The office was responsible for establishing rent control, price control, and rationing policy, writing detailed regulations . . . and promulgating them in the Field . . . OPA's term for the rest of the country." At OPA she met Bob Treuhaft, an enforcement attorney, whose job it was to ban all driving except for business reasons. He'd written the regs on pleasure driving. Having both been from the school that holds "they govern best that govern everything," the attraction was immediate. That he was handsome and brilliant and Jewish and from the Bronx and well left of the ordinary New Dealers there, and that her father could be counted on to disapprove, made the match all the more dear. They married, settled in California, joined the Communist Party. He worked for the trade unions. She had sons, first Nicholas, then Benjamin. When he was ten, Nicholas was killed when a bus hit him on his bicycle half a block from their home in Oakland. "We went dysfunctional," the siblings both say now. "We couldn't talk to each other. We never talked about it again. It was as if Nicky was eradicated from the family." The dead boy's older sister wore a red pleated dress to his funeral. She remembers that, and people milling around and a sense of total despair. "It's all blocked out," the younger brother says when asked about his memories of it. As Benjamin and Constancia explain it now, Decca, being a Communist, did not believe in "that pie in the sky when you die thing," and being from her class and times, she had no faith in psychology. She thought it was a rip-off, according to Dinky. With no god to get mad at and no doctor to talk to and a ban on talk within the family, "we did our best but we didn't do very well." Constancia was thirteen, Benjamin seven, when Nicky was killed in 1954.

"To trace the origins of this book," Jessica Mitford writes in the introduction to the *Revisited* text, "my husband, Bob Treuhaft, got fired up on the subject of the funeral industry in the mid-to-late 1950s."

Decca joined the effort—what she called her "frontal assault on one of the seamier manifestations of American capitalism." Her first article on the subject, called "St. Peter Don't You Call Me," was published in 1958. This was not about fighting the Fascists and the Nazis and the forces of evil, of course, but, in her words, "the undertakers were an easy target" and, as she wrote further, *The American Way of Death* allowed her to "give full rein to [her] subversive nature."

Of course, it never had as much to do with death—in the eternal-question sense of the word—as with dollars. It was the business, and in particular the American way of business, that mostly bothered her—that market-driven, mid-century ma-and-pa capitalism, whereby folks were free to make a million and likewise free to starve; where the haves and have-nots were divided, not, in the mannerly British style, by class and caste but by black and white.

And if I read the papers right, there is a preferred British way.

The notices in *The Daily Telegraph* make it plain. Most everyone in Britain dies peaceably, in hospital, after a brief illness. There are, of course, the sad exceptions. One unfortunate dies "tragically whilst walking in the Dolomites." One "slipped her moorings" and another "went to sleep in her garden." Another is said to have bravely kept her sense of humor—well, *humour*—but it's all the same. The facts of death in late-century England are like the facts of death on the rest of the planet, down all of its history—to wit, it happens.

In this way these classified announcements are the same, always and everywhere—declaratives of births or deaths or marriages, the things we used to get only one of, heavy on the adverbials, with the surnames in boldface and the dates and places and particulars spelled out. It is the small print in every newspaper, paid for, by the line, by the families of the internationally unknown folks who don't merit an obit—the larger biographical homages paid to actresses and admirals and anyone else the editor deems newsworthy that appear with file photos on the next page free of charge.

What strikes me as particularly British is how these notices not only tell the reader what has happened but also what one may or mustn't do about it. Of the dozens of deaths announced on any given day, most instruct "no flowers" or "family flowers only." One family, which apparently approves of flowers while abhorring flowermongers, will allow "garden or wildflowers only." Would the new Princess Diana Memorial Rose just launched by Jackson & Perkins, with the full approval of Princess Di's estate, qualify? It is, as the senior vice-president of marketing and merchandising says, "a classic hybrid tea. Its ivory petals are overlaid with a clear pink blush, and the large, elegantly shaped buds open into graceful, full flowers with impeccable form and a sweet fragrance." And 15 percent of its retail goes toward the Princess Diana Memorial Fund.

Another family feels duty bound to tell folks how to dress for the Thanksgiving service to which everyone is welcome but "no black ties." Presumably a Thanksgiving service is one at which such possibly untidy outpourings as sympathy, good riddance, rage, guilt or abject grief would be as out of place as black ties or the dead body or any of the other dour accoutrements of death. You may be grateful but not aggrieved. Still another family will have no funeral, no flowers and "no letters, please," in anticipation of that vexing custom among the upper crust to send handwritten heart-rending notes when someone dies. They have spent a little more than fifteen pounds per line to announce that the only appropriate response to this fellow's death is a donation to St. Paul's. Indeed, these notices, while tough on florists, provide a litany of the accounts into which one's respects might most properly be paid: Cancer Research, asthma and Alzheimer's, the Injured Jockeys Fund, hospitals and hospices and heart foundations. I wonder if all that money saved on flowers is really spent on cancer cures or church repairs. I wonder how many citizens just go out and spend their commemorative dosh on pints of lager or a couple of gins consoling themselves: "The old boy wouldn't want us to be morbid after all!" And sometimes I wonder just how it would look if someone specified "just send roses" or "only yellow mums" or "in lieu of donations, just drink merlot in memory of our beloved so and so." Would we notice then the bad form of telling people what they should and shouldn't do when it comes to the reasonable expressions of grief or empathy or fellow feelings?

Of course, these notices, and the families who place them, are only trying to be helpful. And if they err on the side of privacy, the stiff upper lip, continence and control, well, what could be more, well, British, eh? Ms. Mitford favored cost efficiency, good causes and geographical cures: "the day after the baby was buried" she writes of her infant daughter's death, "we left for Corsica. There we lived for three months in the welcome unreality of a foreign town, shielded by distance from the sympathy of friends." Welcome unreality of foreign towns, indeed.

Maybe Evelyn Waugh, no sympathetic witness for the dismal trades, had it right when he wrote: "I sniff in Miss Mitford's jolly book . . . a resentment that anyone at all (except presumably writers) should make any money out of anything. The presence of death makes the activities of undertakers more laughable, but I feel she would have the same scorn for hatters or restaurateurs."

Still, *The American Way of Homburgs* or *Hamburgers* wouldn't cause much stir. Even *The American Way of Birth,* which Mitford offered up eight years ago, was pretty much ignored. But *The American Way of Death,* published thirty-seven years ago, went through printing after printing, was the subject of TV specials and was responsible for major shifts in the way people disposed of their dead and marked their passings. The cremation rate in the

United States rose from 3 percent to 22 percent. The Federal Trade Commission passed regulations against the "package deals" most mortuaries sold decades ago. And the range of available options, consumer information and mandated disclaimers has expanded remarkably since Ms. Mitford began her inquiries.

That expanded choices and brisk competition bring with them the possibility of bad choices and abusive sales schemes seemed to catch Ms. Mitford by surprise. The new, if not improved, *Revisited* edition articulates her outrage at the marketing of cremation services and products, the pre-need sales scams, the "bottom-line" mentality of new corporate giants buying up family owned and operated funeral homes around the globe.

A new chapter, titled "A Global Village of the Dead," details the hard-sell abuses of SCI (Service Corporation International), the Houston-based conglomerate that operates on several continents. They now handle one in eight deaths in the United Kingdom, one in five in the United States and most mortuaries in Paris and Australia. In London, the royals moved their appointment from Kenyons to Leverton & Sons when the former was bought out by SCI. "Of all the changes in the funeral scene over the last decades," Decca writes, "easily the most significant is the emergence of monopolies in what the trade is pleased to call the 'death care' industry." And she is right. Economies of scale that trade on "bigger is better" models of merger and acquisition and see every sadness as a sales-op often leave the consumer out in the cold. But she is blind to the coincidence of big-business invasions (which she abhors) and big-government involvement (which she pioneered) in what was, until Mitford, a small and unexpandable market. Likewise, she fails to notice that cremation, pre-need and cost cutting were notions the marketplace learned from her. Ever ready to trade custom for convenience, to discount meaning for cost efficiency, she fails to recognize her own hand in shaping the future of a "death-care" marketplace that has been "Mitfordized."

Indeed, the impact of *The American Way of Death* on the custom and culture of funeral practices in this country is the very reason why this *Revisited* edition fails to surprise, alarm or seem much more than old news retold, repackaged and resold. Folks still bury and burn their dead with ceremony and Jessica Mitford still thinks it costs too much. She has uncovered, for a new generation of what she reckons are guilt-ridden, grief-disabled, easily confused consumers, that funeral directors sell caskets for more than what they pay for them. She has probed their trade journals and infiltrated their conventions to find them unopposed to profit. And she exposes that they have merchandising schemes to induce the consumer to buy what they are selling. In this they are like stockbrokers, oncologists, booksellers and publishers, retailers of Beanie Babies and Viagra, preachers and psychologists, realtors and optometrists, senators, celebrities and the purveyors of Sunday papers and *The Daily News*.

Which is not to say the old read is not still a good laugh. It is, of course—Mitford was nothing if not a wit. "Death Warmed Over" is what she planned to call this book, but really "*Decca* Warmed Over" is nearer the mark. Because the book, finished by a committee of Decca-come-latelies and Jessica Wanna-bes, retains her biases but lacks her style. Still, there are flashes of her deft raillery: the one about the undertaker who tells the customer she will have to buy a more expensive casket because the corpse is too tall for the one she chose, and when the client balks he says he'll just have to cut off the feet. And all that fun over the oxy-moronic mortuary-speak she turned up in their catalogs: the "Practical Burial Footwear Company," and the "Futurama—the casket styled for the future."

"Decca would do anything for a laugh," Dinky says. She knew that a good laugh gets more company than a good cry; and whistling past the graveyard sells better than going in. And going in is something she could never do. Of the American way of death, what put her off the most is this tendency to mark our losses and grieve our dead in ways that she could never understand, and to measure the worth of such endeavors by something other than the retail costs.

One can only speculate—as Dinky and Benji and I tried to do—on what she'd think of the multimedia, intercontinental extravaganzas held in California and London that marked her death. Committees were formed and money was raised and halls were engaged and music was selected and speakers were arranged, and a good cause was named for memorial contributions. (Benjamin's "Send a Piana to Havana" project raised ten thousand, according to Dinky.) In London they rented the Lyric Theatre in Shaftesbury Avenue at a cost, one reckons, exponentially higher than any "average" funeral. But for the hundreds of those who loved her and attended, from Maya Angelou to Salman Rushdie, to her husband and her daughter and her son, the services had meaning and comforts beyond the invoices. For this was a woman who was admired and celebrated and loved, really truly loved, for all her passions and causes and foibles. To have done nothing would have been simpler, easier, more convenient and cheaper—a good bargain on a bad deal. So something had to be done. Not because it matters to the dead, but because the dead matter to the living.

Sadly, Decca hadn't the range for such contemplations. A writer who offers two books called *The American Way of Death* and never mentions the names of her two children who died can be called quirky or eccentric or private or brave. But a woman who writes two volumes of autobiography and never discusses these facts of her life can only be called silent, sad and silent. After all the blathering and good-humored banter, it is that silence that nearly deafens now. The American way of death for Decca was to do the math, not the mourning. To concentrate on money and keep the mysteries at bay. "She preferred," as *The Independent* said in her obituary, "never to speak of it." As if the mention of these hurts might unleash those difficult, untidy, terribly American feelings she would not allow herself and disapproved of in others. Prices were not the only things she labored to control. The numbing drone of numbers had, for her, its comforts.

So here are some numbers for whatever they're worth:

A funeral that cost under a thousand dollars thirty-five years ago now costs nearly five thousand dollars. A book that cost five bucks back then costs twenty-five today.

Go figure.

The Dead Priest

My father was twelve when his uncle, the priest, died. My grandfather, the dead priest's brother, took my father along to make the arrangements. There were two funeral homes in Jackson, Michigan, then—one Catholic, one Protestant—and two cemeteries, likewise divided. A road between them separated the obelisks and old rugged crosses from the angels, madonnas and sacred hearts— St. John's Cemetery from Evergreen Municipal. One fence enclosed them both. There were two gates.

While my grandfather was talking plots and requiems with the funeral director, my father found his way downstairs from the parlors to a room in which two men in white shirtsleeves and suspenders were dressing the dead priest in his liturgical vestments. Green chasuble over a white alb. After lifting the body into the full couch casket they put the priest's biretta in one corner of the casket lid, the large daily missal in the other and a chalice and rosary between the lifeless, consecrated hands. Only then did they notice the boy in the corner.

Years later my father would retell this story with a sense of destiny and providence. To his witness of these ministrations, he would always trace his determination to become a funeral director, his occupation. I suppose the only other possible course would have been Holy Orders: a vocation.

Of the fatherhoods available to Irish Catholic men of the age, I'm grateful he chose the one that included the pursuit of my blessed mother and produced my nativity twelve years later.

I was named after the dead priest and baptized by one of his classmates and brother priests who had come to Detroit from his native Galway. Father Kenny later taught me the Latin responses to be said at Mass by the altar boy. I was seven years old when I learned these things. I would go on Tuesday afternoons to the rectory, where I would be schooled in the ancient rubrics: *Introibo ad altare Dei* (I will go in unto the altar of God). *Ad Deum qui laetificat juventutem meam* (To God Who giveth joy to my youth).

Among the joys given to my youth, I was assigned, three weeks out of four, to serve six-twenty A.M. Mass. I would arrive at St. Columban's in the dark with chilled cruets of wine and water, don my cassock and surplice, light two candles for Low Mass, set out the bells, the book, the bowl and the hand towel, and wordlessly assist Father Kenny with his vestments—amice and cincture, stole and maniple. On his signal, we would process out of the sacristy into the sanctuary to an audience of daily supplicants, busy with their beads and votives. We would genuflect in front of the tabernacle. I would kneel. He would begin. We'd trade phrases and prayers. He'd whisper over the bread and wine. I'd ring the bells and hold the golden paten under the chins of the communicants lest any of the sacred species fall. At the conclusion of Mass, after the dispatch of my duties in the sacristy, I was required by Father Kenny to kneel in the back row of the church and give thanks for no less than fifteen minutes. What I was thankful for, I was told, was the Eucharist, the Body and Blood of Our Lord Jesus Christ, and the privilege of assisting at Mass these early mornings. Whenever I'd try to hasten my escape, Father Kenny would return me to the pew with the admonition "Be stingy with the Lord, Tomas"—for he used the Irish version of my name—"and the Lord will be stingy with you." This sounded a lot like "You get what you pay for," which my father was always saying about shoes and cars and accessories; and "quid pro quo," which I later heard as a legal dictum. Unknown to me at the time was a plot hatched between my mother and Father Kenny that would eventuate in my ordination. I'd been named for a priest who had died too young, and it made an odd kind of sense that I should carry out his priesthood. Thus my early education in the parroting of Latin was only a head start of sorts. I loved the sound and meter of the prayers, the Confiteor and Suscipiat, and four decades since I still know those mysterious syllables by heart. And the ancient hymns that were sung, the Pange Lingua, Panis Angelicus, Tantum Ergo and the rest. And, though their literal meanings elude me, the message is the same. I am Catholic in the way I am American and male and Caucasian, by birth. It is like language. Or, more precisely, like a highly specialized dialect of a language I learned because my people spoke it.

My Christianity, such as it is, is a day-to-day matter of choice, a function of intellect and instruction. My Catholicism is impressed, embedded, inexorably a part of my being. It is instinct and intuition. I might cease to believe as one, but I will ever behave and misbehave as one. And while my Christianity linked me to Methodists and Presbyterians and Lutherans and the Orthodox, my Catholicism kept me separate from them. Just as my humanity links me to Buddhists and Jews and Muslims and Secular Humanists, my Christianity separates me from them. Though we may, in fits of tolerance and insight, allow as how we are all God's children, a reoccurring doctrine of every religion seems to be that its adherents are the favorite sons and darlingmost daughters. This is a bone of contention over which we have fought since Cain and Abel and, more recently, between Christians and Muslims, Israelis and Palestinians, Ulster Catholics and Ulster Protestants. Down history we have been willing to kill and die over which Sunday was Easter, which primate was pope, which prophet was crazed and which inspired. We have burned witches, plundered countries, with God on our side and the Devil on theirs, in the name of every prophet and pope, potentate and saint. History includes the bloody and abundant themes of holocaust and crusade, mission and misunderstanding. Thus we arrive at the mixed blessing of religiosity: that to commit to one religion is to separate from one's larger humanity. Communion with one too often entails exclusion of the others to our detriment and theirs.

Perhaps the best metaphor for this sense of discriminatory community is not the stained-glass window but Microsoft Windows in all of its incarnations, to use the system near to hand. While we can work our way from the highly inclusive, broad-based common denominator of, say, the PC system to the drive and program, through file and folder and document and filter until we come to the address list for the daughter's wedding invitations; in the same way we enter this world unencumbered by definition or bias. To the universe of Creation we are no more specific than *earthling* and thereby have more in common with rhubarb and dolphins than we do with Martians and Venusians. Our oxygen-based vitality separates us from rocks and water, our mammality from the pelicans and black bass, our humanity from zebras and cocker spaniels, our Christianity from the other three quarters of the family of man and my Catholicism from the regular Christians, who never had any use for holy water and bingo and limbo. My Irish (as opposed to Polish or Italian or Korean or Byzantine) Catholicism defines me further still. Each of these filters helps to define and specify and articulate my identity and runs the risk of separating me from the larger community. I can add some of my own. White, Male, Middle-aged, Bumptious, Balding, on and on, until I turn up with my own unique, sui generis, singular self, utterly alone, utterly unlike anyone else.

Often this is when you hear the voice of God, or begin, at least, to listen in earnest.

You may, of course, take exception to this model and I can lay your disagreement to the fact that I am a Rotarian and you are a Kiwanian, or perhaps you are female or Republican or left-handed or young or gay or formerly Yugoslavian. Our differences define us. They make us dear and divided and, by degrees, The Other. Sometimes our opposites attract and fit, and sometimes they fight. They make us passionate in love and hate.

I HAD A NUNNISH UPBRINGING. Catholics at mid-century were fairly ghettoized even in the suburbs, where sameness was the new theme. The church had established parallel institutions for education and health care, as well as for social, fiscal and professional life. Catholics were a culture within a culture. So while my Methodist and Episcopalian pals went off to Torrey School, two blocks north, I got sent on the two-mile walk to Holy Name School, where Sister Servants of the Immaculate Heart of Mary lay in wait for us. These were holy young women in black and blue habits optimally configured to hide their breasts and hair and other, well, attributes. They wore sensible shoes and carried huge rosaries. Often they hid their hands in their sleeves. They'd traded their given names and surnames for religious names that said, I suppose, something about their rich fantasy lives. Sister Jean Pierre, I imagined, imagined a life on the Seine with artists and writers. She taught us French responses to her French queries: *Comprennez-vous? Oui, oui, notre bonne soeur!* She read to us from Valéry and hung Monet prints from the blackboard, and some afternoons she would give us a silent reading assignment and stand at the tall windows, staring out into the greensward, looking distant, transported and unspeakably beautiful. Sister Francis Clare had perfect penmanship and spelling but would sometimes confuse *Francis* with *Frances* in her signature—a fact I uncovered while passing back homework assignments. While acoustically her name paid homage to the great saints of Assisi who kept a cleanly distance between their passions centuries ago, the tendency to spell *Francis* sometimes as a man and other times as a woman made us all believe that the nun suffered night sweats and possibly some gender confusions. It is probably a sin to say that Sister James Edward had a celestial body. To this she added the general temperament of a linebacker to keep our attention focused all through our formative years. She taught religion through *Father McGuire's Baltimore Catechism No.2 Official Revised Edition,* a slim green volume that covered us through Confirmation, at age twelve. It dispensed the particulars of our religion in a numbered question-and-answer format. To wit: "1. Who made us? God made us." Or, "5. From whom do we learn to know, love and serve God? We learn to know, love and serve God from Jesus Christ, the Son of God, who teaches us through the Catholic Church." Or, much later, "425. What are the chief means of satisfying the debt of our temporal punishment, besides the penance imposed after confession? Besides the penance imposed after confession, the chief means of satisfying the debt of our temporal punishment are: prayer, attending Mass, fasting, almsgiving, the works of mercy, the patient endurance of sufferings and indulgences."

None of these women was ever anything but kind to me and each treated me with the dignity due to a child of God, which they insisted I was. From them I learned the diagramming of sentences and the lifelong search for lowest common denominators. I learned about character and conscience. They taught me the discernment of hidden beauties. And if they had some unpopular notions about masturbation and copulation, it is also true that they presented themselves as virgins and martyrs, Brides of Christ, ever in readiness for His coming, cheerfully and blessedly ignorant of or inexperienced in these near occasions of sin. In short, they made no secret of the fact that they didn't know what it was they were talking about. To be sure, they spoke of the mysteries of "petting" and "intercourse" and "self-abuse" in such hushed and blushing ways that it drove us into paroxysms of desire and longing and, some days, into the boys' room during lunch recess to disabuse ourselves of these joyful and glorious mysteries. That most of us lived with parents who were supplying us with new brothers and sisters every eighteen months provided a necessary balance to our daytimes with these immaculate chastitutes.

Sister Jean Thérèse sold pagan babies for five dollars a copy. I bought four with the money from my paper route. I named them after saints and archangels and waited for their letters. This began an early interest in the missions, one that was always encouraged by the nuns and later by the Christian Brothers, who took over my instruction in high school, though, for the latter, encouragement had an air of extortion about it. My sense of calling to this mission proceeded from item 166 in *The Baltimore Catechism:* "Are all obliged to belong to the Catholic Church in order to be saved? All are obliged to belong to the Catholic Church in order to be saved." This meant that not only the pagan babies the nuns were selling us, or the starving people in China for whom we were eating our vegetables ad nauseum, but also my Protestant neighbors were in peril of eternal damnation. I had my work cut out for me. I started with Michael McGaw, next door. It seemed like the neighborly thing to do.

Michael was a lackluster Methodist. His parents were teachers and Democrats who nonetheless voted against Kennedy for reasons their pastor probably never articulated. I told him about the spiritual and corporal works of mercy, thinking that this might get him interested in switching churches and adding to the account I kept with God. When this did not move him, I detailed for him the life of St. Blaise, the patron of sore throats, an Armenian who was beheaded (thus the connection to sore throats) in the fourth century. But after an entire afternoon of building model planes and my discussing purgatory and the fires of hell, Mike told me I was full of shit and if he could put up with a raving Catholic I'd have to put up with him "Just as I am," he said, and winked as if I should know what that meant.

I had a more religious experience with Cathy Shryock, who was a year younger than Mike and me but had shown early signs of maturation. She made it clear she'd like me to evangelize her one Thursday afternoon downstairs by the pocket-pool table in her basement. It changed my life. We were reading together from the *Lives of the Saints*, the illustrated version, which had a saint for every day of the year. It must have been mid-February because I remember her interest in St. Catherine dei Ricci, the sixteenth-century Florentine prioress whose reputation for sanctity was well known to popes and other Romans, not least St. Philip Neri, to whom "she appeared in a most miraculous manner while still alive." She was famous, the text further explained, for "the 'Ecstasy of the Passion' which she experienced every Thursday from noon until Friday at 4 P.M. for twelve years." Cathy and I took to meeting on Thursdays, there in the basement's half-light, for weeks to come, during which she appeared to me in miraculous apparitions full of ecstasy and passion. She taught me to play eight ball and straight pool and kiss like a movie star.

Life seems a pursuit of communion and atonement. To be at one with God and at peace with our neighbors. So much about religion puts us at odds. But at the same time it gives us the gift of language. Faith and fear share the same vocabulary; hope and despair share the same metaphors; love and mistrust trade well-known idioms. I am given a voice by a church that is shaped by famine in Ireland, schism in Byzantium, encyclicals from Rome, crusades to the East, missions to the West. And I have been, as a Catholic, variously devout, lukewarm, outraged and indifferent; comforted, contemptuous, pious and proud; ashamed, lazy, zealous and amazed. I have been, like the church, imperfect, inconsistent, mean-spirited, cruel and loving, and loved.

Like my father, I could not be a priest. I chose a paternity of flesh and blood and have never been happily celibate for long. Indeed, the celibacy that made priests emblems of transcendent humanity half a century ago today makes them suspect and distant. An irony is that so inspired a theology of life can translate into such uninspired notions of living, especially with regard to our sexuality.

And in my fatherhood, I have paid more attention to the spiritual than the religious lives of my children. If the gift of my upbringing was certainty, the gift of theirs seems more like wonder. If I was ever a very good Catholic, they will be all the more catholic. Their world will be smaller, their heaven larger.

And also like my father, I chose an undertaking that put me in earshot of several dialects of the larger tongue. I bury the dead. I dress them and put them in caskets and take them to church. The colloquies of love and grief, life and death, suffering and salvation, in my work, achieve a kind of harmony, a kind of silence. I've heard it from Southern Baptists and High Church Anglicans and Humanists and Unitarians and Missouri Synod Lutherans and Evangelicals of every kind. I have buried Christian Scientists and Mormons and Jehovah's Witnesses and Church of Christ and Dutch Reform and Romanian Orthodox and Chaldean Christians. I've buried Jews and Zen Buddhists and Rastas and Hopis. And priests and pastors and nuns and brothers. We take our leave, much as we came, unencumbered by doctrine, speechless, miraculous and natural.

Fish Stories

I taught my son to fish when he was four. It was a pond in West-chester County, New York. We'd gone there from Michigan to visit his mother's family. I brought a bass rod with an ultralight spinning reel, hooks and sinkers and bobbers. We dug worms. I cast out the line and hand-ed him the pole and launched into the usual preachments on Patience. I hadn't ten words out of my mouth when the red-and-white bobber started popping, the line tightened and the pole shook and Tommy, without further instruction, set the hook and reeled in a bluegill the size of my hand. My first son's first fish.

He held the thing, still hooked, both of them round-eyed and gaping in amazement, both of them gulping the blue air in each other's face. He was hooked. He wanted to take it and show his mother.

I said if he took it to show his mother it would die and we would eat it. Or we could put it back in the pond and it could go see its own fish mother and tell her about the boy it'd caught and it would live to get bigger and bigger and bigger. "No, Dad," he said, he'd just go show his mother. He didn't want to eat it. He'd just go show his mother and come right back and send it back to its mother and everything would be right with the world. But I told him the fish couldn't live out of the water. It couldn't breathe out of the water. It would die out of the water. It was in its nature.

He wanted to keep it. And he didn't want it to die. And I could see in his bright blue eyes the recognition that these aims were at cross-purposes. This was a game he couldn't play for "keeps." He was crying when he put it back in the water. Catch and release, like love and grief, are difficult notions. We've been fishing together ever since.

I know you're thinking that's cute enough to make you puke. I know you're thinking to yourself, Oh, sure, I'll bet—bluegill, blue eyes, the blue day in Westchester County. But it's true. He was hooked.

After that it was carp fishing on Sunday mornings at the secret spot south of town. We'd pack soggy Raisin Bran around big treble hooks and heave it out and let it sit on the bottom until some old carp would come and suck it up. Tommy was a carp-killing boy. And long after I learned to sleep in on Sundays, he'd bike out to the secret spot and kill carp all spring and summer and bring them home to plant them in the garden, where now, near twenty years since, the perennials grow thick and hardy and fishy. Once I remember him golden among a dozen shorter admirers returning from fishing with a carp the size of a small child hanging from his handlebars, blood and creamy milt oozing from it, its tail dragging in the dust and all of his amazed compatriots poking it and holding their noses and putting forth a frenzy of questions. "What kind? How big? How long the fight? Was it dead?" And even the one some noisy boyo advanced about the white substance proceeding from the dead carp's lower parts, to which Tommy replied, as if he knew what it meant, "Spawning." They took him at his word. In just such ways young boys get attached to trophies.

Then he got crazy for bass and pike and all the other pan fish that habited the inland lakes around our town. Arbogast Bug-eyes, and Fat Rapallas and plastic worms in every flavor filled his tackle box. He'd fish mornings before school and afternoons after school and show up at home shortly after dark smelly and content. He never excelled at his studies much.

When he was nine I took him to the Pere Marquette—the long river in western Michigan named for the French Jesuit who died in its estuary. It was early March. It was freezing. But the river, working its ninety-mile way west from Baldwin to its eventual spillage into Lake Michigan at Ludington, never slowed enough to ice over. We hiked in, in Red Ball waders and snowmobile suits, through the snow and frozen swamp. I remember holding him up, afloat, his left hand high in my right hand, like dancers, to keep him from dipping his waders through deeper spots in the river bottom. The place we fished was called Gus's Hole because the man who showed me the spot some years before had called it that. We drifted spawn bags on long light leaders below split shot through gravel runs and a deep sandy hole for winter-run steelhead and resident browns. It was here Tommy learned to distinguish the tick of the tiny sinkers moving through stones from the bite of fish. It was here the topography of the riverbed began to make sense to him. He could close his eyes and see the bottom, its undulant waterscape of runs and pools and holes and flats, the pockets of curling water, the structure of tree stumps and rock forms, the gravel beds where fish would hold, the shaded and the sunlit water. The only fish caught that day was an eighteen-inch brown trout, beautifully speckled. All fathers pray for their sons to outfish them. My prayers were answered and have been answered ever since.

That September we went back to the Pere Marquette to fish the salmon run. I explained, I suppose, how they went upstream to spawn and die—how everything in nature replicates itself then disappears. I thought he might have further questions on this theme and figured the river was a good place to discuss them. But he was more concerned with the relative attractions of Mepps spinners, Little Cleos and the assortment of streamers and flies he had brought with him. He caught two beauties, two big fresh males, fishing deep gravel between two sunken logs at Gleeson's Landing.

I have a picture of his boyhood in my mind that shows him standing upright between these two huge fish he is trying to hold aloft that weigh near half as much as he does. Half-wince, half-grin, his face is all effort and capability. Behind him it is late September—scrub pines, cedar and winter oak—the air is golden with possibilities, the river is silver, the smell of leaf fall and blood sport is everywhere and he is happy because we are taking his trophies home to show his mother. And I must be nearby holding the camera, trying to keep this moment permanent, in tact, coaxing him always "Smile, Tommy, smile!"

I used to think that it was trying to replicate this moment, this very picture, there between his trophies, that has kept him fishing ever since. That perfect autumn before his mother and father were divorced, the river thick with chinook and coho, his grandparents still alive, there in the bronze light of that September, still years before a girl he loved in school would grow into a woman and leave town and marry someone else, there in his waders, nine and smiling, the blissful ignorance of a boyhood undisturbed by love and grief, sex and death, the heart's divisions between catch and release.

But I was wrong. It was not my son who was trying to save it. It was me. It was my image of his childhood—that innocence—my hopeless efforts to spare him heartache, my own stupidity, my own daft fears of this life's opposites. He was never afraid of these things. Like everything in nature, he was laboring to know them better.

I am the age my father was when I was my son's age. Figure that: halfway between the middle half-century between those two. Sometimes it seems that we repeat ourselves. Time seems a constant game of catch and release. Dream and vision, memory and reflection—each is an effort to hold life still, like paintings of fruit and flowers on a table. There is no still life. My son's youth, my age, my father's death—each is a marvel of time and motion. Each becomes the other, endlessly.

And, like everything in nature, salmon bear their share of existential lessons. In the autumn all they do is spawn and die. They return to the exact water of their own making undistracted by the smaller details. They do not feed. It is not hunger that makes them crush a caddis or stone fly in their bony jaw; it is rage.

"Imagine," Tom once told me, "you're getting it on with the one true love of your life, your one and only. And this is quite literally the one you will die for, and you're making progress and someone keeps ringing the doorbell with a pizza you never even ordered, and you're trying to stay focused because you've come a long way to do this and you've never had any practice and you're only going to get this one shot and then it's curtains and the goddamn doorbell keeps ringing and someone shouting at you 'Pizza's here!' and all you can think of is how you're not hungry and didn't order anything and you're busy at the moment with the meaning of life and now this asshole's banging on the door shouting 'Pizza!' and you'd do anything to make him disappear because you've really got important things to do here and he keeps on ringing and banging and shouting until all you can think of to do is kill him. I tie my flies," he said, "not to look like pizza, but to look like the delivery guy."

Such wisdoms as these ought not be forgotten.

The hens find home gravel, fanning it clean with their huge tails before they deposit their abundant roe among the stones. The bucks find spawning hens, behind whom they hold in the current waiting for the moment of their ejaculation. The hens' dance makes the bucks dance wildly until, crazy with the kind of blind desire young men relate to and old men remember, they spend themselves entirely. By this point in the process, they have begun to die. Their fins whiten, their bodies darken, they get toothy and tired and make for the slow backwater pools and shallows.

The English poet laureate Ted Hughes, who died himself one recent October, and knew some things about death and desire, wrote it well when he wrote in "October Salmon" thus:

Now worn out with her tirelessness, her insatiable quest,
Hangs in the flow, a frayed scarf—

An autumnal pod of his flower,
The mere hull of his prime, shrunk at shoulder and flank,

In the October light
He hangs there, patched with leper-cloths.

All this, too, is stitched into the torn richness,
The epic poise
That holds him so steady in his wounds, so loyal to his doom,
    so patient
In the machinery of heaven.

Boys, of course, know sex when they see it. So do girls. And they know death. And standing in the Pere Marquette, my son has seen a lot of each. The river in October is full of the sweet air of desire and putrefaction—silver fish, full of life's aching, making their fierce way upriver. Dark fish, their duties spent, float belly-up downstream, lodge in the log jams, rotting, dead.

We must all be steady in our wounds, loyal to our doom, patient in the machinery of heaven.

Having taught him to fish, now he teaches me. He rows me down the river, through the deep holes and gravel runs, and shows me what to cast and where to cast it.

He works the river for a living now. He has a drift boat, a regular clientele and hard-won expertise. He ties his own flies, packs shore lunches for his customers, ties their knots and nets their fish, and coaches them, as he still coaches me, on the intricacies of pattern and presentation and the river bottom, on the structure of currents that can't be seen, the epic poise, and on the catching of salmon and their release.

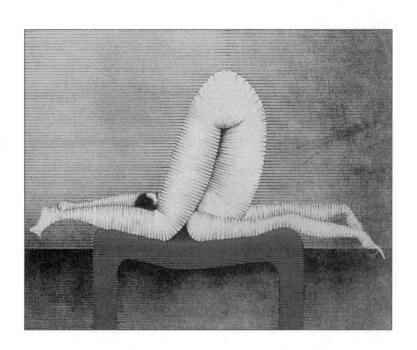

The Blindness of Love

I'd like to leave you in love's blindness,
cherish the comfort of your art, the way
it makes me whole and shining
—FROM "NOT YOUR MUSE,"
BY PAULA MEEHAN

That born-again First Baptist notion of a Personal Savior is one that has troubled me all my life. The thought that whomever we have to thank for the weather and the Internet and the cosmos would likewise keep track of the hairs on my head—an easier duty as life goes on—is troubling and wonderful.

Astronauts return from space convinced of the glory and grandeur of Creation. It is no less so when one witnesses nativity firsthand, or looks into the void of death.

In all that is and is not, the Hand of God is manifest.

But the notion that the Maker of It All is also the caretaker, confidant, someone to go to in a pinch, when the luck's run out and you're up against it—that's a dodgier concept, on the order of suggesting that Bill Gates gives a rap about the trouble you're having while doing up the wedding invites on Microsoft Publisher. Go ahead. Give the twenty-four-hour help line a call. Ask for Bill. See what happens.

And I'm always suspect of the party line that holds there's only one way to get to Heaven, or one class of people certain to be there, or one creed or confession that has the goods on God—whomever He or She is these days.

Mightn't God answer to all our names and speak all our languages and count all our efforts at understanding worthy? "The sun," we say, or "the moon," but in truth ours is *a* sun and there are millions of moons. Oughtn't such deconstruction work with "the Way, the Truth, the Light?"

Still, the way it happened to me, when I was up against it, you know, hapless, damaged, looking into the void, it was as if Whoever Is in Charge Here said, "This man needs *that* good woman in his life." Not "*a* good woman"—of which there has never been a shortage. But "*that* good woman"—of whom there is this only one.

That's what made it seem, well, personal—a personal save—the one with my name on it since the beginning of time just waiting for me to walk in out of the blue and say I'm ready now.

Mind you, we had both spent many years, all of our lives, really, demonstrating our ability to live without each other. And each of us brought a fair bit of "baggage." And each of us could survive, maybe even thrive, without the other. And no one knows what the future holds.

But when I look into her eyes I see the blindness of love. That's the gift. It is not darkness. It is a vision. She sees me in the way Whoever Is in Charge Here meant me to be seen. She sees me better than I see myself.

One little example—I promise, only one.

We had the poet Paula Meehan visiting from Dublin. She was reading at the university on the midwestern leg of a national tour. She was staying with us for a couple of days.

It's Sunday. I'm reading the Sunday paper. In the next room Paula and my One and Only are watching the movie version of Jim

Harrison's novella called *Legends of the Fall*. Maybe you've seen it—
Sir Anthony Hopkins, Brad Pitt, Montana—the usual suspects. And
everything is as it should be. I'm reading the obits. The kids are all out
on their various rounds. Paula and My True Love are drinking cups
of tea on the couch, smoking cigarettes with impunity, watching old
movies on the TV. And there's this quiet little hum of their conversation, two lovely bookish women in their primes, two rich internal lives
alive in the next room, and the sunlight through the window and big
music gathering in the background on the video and the absence of
the names of anyone I love in the obits in the Sunday paper and I'm
thinking "This is the day the Lord has made—let us be glad and
rejoice!" or kindly sentiments to that effect when all of a sudden I
hear this whooping and hollering and hoopla in the next room.

"Yippee! Ky Ay Ky Ay!"

"Ride 'em, cowboy!"

"Yes, oh yes, get along little doggie . . ."

So I drop what I'm reading and come on the run.

And there they are—Paula and My Darling—up off the
couch, up on their tiptoes, their mouths wide open, their arms flail-
ing in the air the way you see fans at the World Cup or buyers on
Wall Street or the studio audience on those trash TV shows, and they
are oohing and ahhing and saying "Yes, yes, yes," and there is something vaguely animal in their eyes, something way past reason or
regret, and on the TV I notice it has come to the part where Julia
Ormond (who bears more than a little semblance to the Love of
My Life) has come west from back east to meet the brothers and
the father of the man she's betrothed to—a fine young fellow who
is going to die tragically in the war—and this is the part where they're
coming across the prairie, the whole entourage, Julia and her fiancé
and one of the brothers—some chatty, tight-assed, buttoned-down

upright citizen who, it will turn out, is badly smitten and will make a million dollars and never really satisfy her—and Sir Anthony is looking fatherly and the brothers are looking brotherly and Julia is looking transcendently off in the distance where the camera pans toward Brad Pitt, whose name is Tristan in the movie, and he's coming across the cinematography on his chestnut horse all leather and recklessness and more hair than I or any of the men in my family will ever have blowing in the breeze behind him and Montana—the wild mountains and rivers and valleys and the blue day like a benediction saying this is our beloved one—and that shit-eatin' grin Brad is always flashing because he's trying to pretend that he doesn't really know that any woman in the forty-eight contiguous states, hell, any woman on the planet, would do whatever he asked her to, right there and then, right here and now, because he is the one who is at one with nature and the landscape and wild horses and bear and because though he might be saddle-broken he'll never be tame.

And Paula and My Sweetheart are going weak with the vision. They are holding their ribs and rocking a little and the look on their faces between pleasure and pain, between aching and abandon, is the look I've seen on only a handful of intimate occasions and I'm more than a little worried by now—because the calm, the quiet, the Sunday morning, the day the Lord has made, has gone wanton and astray—and out of my ignorance all I can think of to say is, "Who does he remind you of, my dear?"

And turning toward me with her two brown eyes, slowly, deliberately, like she wants me to believe it, like she wants me never to forget it, like she wants me to feel free to go back to the paper on the table in the next room, like she and Paula can be left alone, she says in the voice I know is hers, "Why, you, my darling, only you."

Funerals-R-Us

"**K**atharine, we die."
The line still startles with its stark economy. It is a line from a poem by a man who, like most poets, could be said to be "internationally ignored." The poem in which this line occurs is called "For Katharine, 1952–1961" and appears in *New & Selected Poems* by Conrad Hilberry, which is the name of the poet who wrote the book. He might never be on *Oprah*. There will not be a movie version or book signings broadcast on C-SPAN II. It was never reviewed in *The New York Times* or on NPR.

It's a brief, heartbreaking, life-affirming poem—a grieving father trying to explain death to his dead daughter ten years after she has died. And, measured against the fat lines of Walt Whitman or Marianne Moore, it is a tiny line: three words only, four syllables, five if you say it slow—fourteen letters, a comma and a full stop—over almost before you know it. One short line of a short poem in a short book published by a respectable university press some years ago—a line which, nonetheless, contains, by all accounts, fully half of all the Existential Truths.

Listen up: *We die!* The other half echoes in the utterance of the first, of course: *We live!* Against one or the other of these two facts all of the other facts of life and death are shaped and reshaped, so that *Morior* (more so than *Cogito*) *ergo sum* is primal among the proofs of our being. *I die, therefore I am.*

I am always trying to imagine the particulars—that first Neanderthal widow waking to the dead lump of her man, somewhere in the Urals or the Apennines, one gray morning forty or fifty thousand years ago. His body has about it a stillness she has not seen in him before. He is dumbstruck, unresponsive in ways that worry her. Changed utterly.

Did she wait until he began to smell? Hours in warm weather, maybe days in winter. Or did she know a dead thing when she saw it—seeing in him what she'd seen before in other formerly living, breathing things. Either way, sooner or later she knew something would have to be done. She could leave the cave to him, his tomb. Or she could dig a hole or build a fire or shove him over the hill or into a ditch or a swamp or the sea. But there would have to be an effort made to budge or bury or burn him up, something involving the larger muscles; and looking up or down or out or into whatever void she would consign him to she would ask herself some sensible questions: *Why is he cold? Is that all there is? Can it happen to me?*

And it was ever thus—all down the history of the species, death was first and foremost an existential experience, the trigger for the overwhelming questions. *What's next?* she must have wondered; and the life of faith and doubt was kindled in humankind. Death and grief, along with sex and love, were and remain chief among the reasons why poets and high priests, shamans and soothsayers, held forth, and why cabinetmakers and livery men, sextons and sin eaters, evolved into the mortuary trades. How much of what we do, from the ridiculous to the sublime, would not be done if we did not die? In the blank face of mortality we always ask, *What's next?*

BURYING MRS. ROBERTSON last April in West Highland Cemetery, I heard it again. It was Mrs. Robertson's son, Alastair, who was asking. His mother had died the sad but timely death, after eighteen months of struggle and constricting existence following a stroke. She was almost eighty. I'd buried her husband five years before. Mr. Robertson had had the acute myocardial infarction men of his generation prayed for—the Big One they reckoned was better than cancer. Alastair, divorced, distanced from his children by their mother's life and their own young adulthoods, quit his condo and moved home with his widowed mother. She cooked. He drove her to church on Sundays. He even began dating a woman who rang bells in the bell choir there. She'd come and do his mother's hair. He'd take her to the movies. Romance blushed, then bloomed, then withered. After his mother's stroke, he had difficult choices. He was fiftyish, fastidious about his investments. He decided to take an early retirement from Ford. He wanted to take care of his mother. There were speech therapists, physical therapists. She'd shown promising early signs of recovery. For whatever reasons, progress slowed, then stalled; hope dimmed, the convalescence turned into a vigil and, in the end, she died, quietly in her own bed, her son nodding in the chair beside her, and Alastair called me in the middle of the night.

My brother and I drove out in the hearse to get her. Alastair had made fresh coffee and written out a brief obituary. He gave us her dress and shoes and pearls and Bible. He helped us carry her down the stairs on the stretcher, and in the front hall he bent to kiss her forehead before we took her to the car. He had her laid out at the funeral home for two nights. Folks came to pay their respects, trade stories, laugh and weep, hug and leave. Then we took her to church, where her pastor and her choir did their parts, and then to West Highland Cemetery, where her body was committed to the ground and her spirit to God, and Rev. Harris tossed the first bit of dirt in the grave, saying "dust to dust," then gave the shovel to Alastair, who did the same and passed the shovel to his kin, who had all come home from their various lives and locales for the services.

It was walking back to the car when Alastair asked me, "Well, Tom, what's next?"

I didn't know exactly what he was asking. Was it the Big Question? You know, about his mother, her future? Did she now occupy the Presbyterian heaven she'd always kept faith in, a cross between Oban and the Florida Keys, with crocheted doilies on the davenport and neighbors from her childhood and old friends from her school days and her family, long gone and grinning from their heavenly mansions as she made her way among them at long last? Had the mortal put on immortality? Was he asking me that? Or was it the Medium-sized Question about his own prospects at fifty-five, unemployed, unmarried, seemingly unnecessary to anyone now, uncertain about his future? Was he posing the rhetorical *what's next* for him? Or was it the Ordinary Question? Do we go back to church now for teas and cakes and ices?

"What's next?" he wondered. And I wondered too.

It was Howard Raether, arguably the last half-century's most informed source on matters mortuary, who wrote years ago that a funeral should *"serve the living by caring for the dead."* It has always seemed to me a sensible measure. And walking back to the cars from Mrs. Robertson's grave, I reckoned hers had done just that. It got her where she needed to be and got her son where he needed to be: to the brink of the life he would lead without her.

Jessica Mitford would have thought it cost too much. In the face of death she mostly wondered, "How much?" Close to six thousand is what I charged Alastair Robertson. Three grand for our services and facilities and cars, a little more than two for the oak casket and cement vault, six hundred for the sexton to open the grave and put up the tent, and the rest on flowers and newspaper notices and tax.

Mitford and Raether used to go toe-to-toe. She wrote *The American Way of Death* and was critic-in-chief of the mortuary trades. He was the executive director of the National Funeral Directors Association for thirty-five years, a lawyer by training and the funeral's chief defender. Back in the sixties they would fight it out on radio and TV and in print interviews. She'd talk money. He'd talk meaning. He'd do values. She'd do costs. She said the funeral was "barbaric display." He said the funeral was "for the living." They disagreed on almost everything. She died in the summer of 1996. He died in October 1999. Both of them worked and wrote and reasoned till the end. Their old contentions still shape the meaning and marketing of American funerals.

IN THE LAST THIRD OF THE LAST CENTURY of this millennium—say, between the deaths of President Kennedy and his son, John—something essential has changed in the conversation about death and grief and funerals. As with life and love, the list of factors and influences is endless: increased mobility, changes in family life and family structure, gender wars, religious indifference, global warming and cable TV. There are seventy-five million baby boomers— in their thirties and forties and early fifties now. The ways we live and love and die and memorialize have changed. We divorce and abort more, cremate and *kevork* more. We roll our own orthodoxies, do our spiritualities buffet-style and, in the way we thought we reinvented sex in the sixties, there is the sense that we are reinventing death at century's end. We're into choices and changes and traveling light.

I've been watching these changes from the corner of First Street and Liberty Boulevard in a small town in the Midwest, where I've been the funeral director for over twenty-five years. It's our family's work. My brothers and sisters and I grew up washing cars and carting flowers, swinging the door and grinning at the puns and entendres of our friends and classmates, working for our father. Some of us went to mortuary school and learned to embalm. Others studied social work, accountancy, liberal arts. As more and more of us chose funeral service as a way of life, the enterprise expanded. There are four funeral homes now that bear the family name in different suburban locations. Of my parents' nine children, all but two work in one of these places.

My town is typical: postindustrial, postmodern, unabashedly postcardish—a Main Street, a weekly newspaper, a population that, for the most part, agrees this is a great place to raise children. We have, along with our Rockwellian images of early-century values and mid-century calm, the late-century storms of drugs and homicides and suicides. In this we are very modern. And there are deaths by all the usual causes too—the cancers and the cardiac arrests and lapses of caution that do us in—a couple of hundred every year. In this way we are timeless, one with the ancients who wondered what to do. When someone dies they call our funeral home.

They still call us in the middle of the night. In such dark times the concerns are immediate and elemental. And I think at such times it has less to do with our shiny hearse and family cars, our newly decorated lounge with the kitchen and cozy parlor or our sponsorship of the church calendars and Little League uniforms; less to do with our price list or casket selection, our parking lot or payment terms, and everything to do with the fact that when they call we answer—no voice mail or automated answering system, no menu of options, no pound keys to push—just someone listening on the other end who will take the sad particulars and drive out in the dark when there is trouble. It's what we do. Our name is on the sign.

LYNCH & SONS is what it says. FUNERAL DIRECTORS.

While most Main Streets across the country—the retailers and realtors, bankers and pharmacists, lawyers and doctors—were all consolidating and snuggling under new computer systems and corporate covers, funeral homes remained, for the most part, stubbornly independent family businesses. While generally abhorred for their proximity to the dead and their trade in grief and mourning, and perennially an easy target for the media in need of outrage or black humor, funeral directors are locally well known and admired for their compassion and capabilities. "They're all crooks," the conventional wisdom holds, "but ours. The one in our town is really very good."

Of the twenty-two thousand funeral homes across the country, 85 percent are still family-owned enterprises that have spent an average of fifty-four years in their communities building their reputations, spending a meager 3 percent of their total income on advertising, relying on goodwill and the reputation of the family name. Maybe this has to do with the one-to-a-customer rule for funerals that still prevails. Or the fact that we shop for them infrequently. Maybe it's because we can't return the damaged or unused portion for replacement. Once broken a funeral is hard to fix, and we want to know who is accountable to us. For these and other reasons, the funeral remains a unique enterprise that resists standardization, classification, downsizing, convenience and efficiencies and most marketing strategies. It relies more on trust, personal attention and accountability.

Now all of that is changing rapidly. Open any copy of *The Director* or the *American Funeral Director*—journals you won't find in your dentist's or internist's waiting room—or drop into any NFDA convention, last autumn in Kansas City, this fall in Baltimore, and you will find that two topics dominate the conversation in funeral service today: consolidation by publicly traded multinational corporations of formerly independent businesses, and preneed sales—the capital-gathering engine that drives these acquisitions and assures a corner on the future market share.

Service Corporation International, the Loewen Group and Stewart Enterprises—the Big Three of the McFuneral Crowd—have been buying up funeral homes and cemeteries and crematories around the world. And while most of the activity in the United States has centered on California, Florida, Texas and the larger metroplexes, these "multinationals" are ever on the lookout to form new "clusters"—networks of funeral homes geographically configured to allow for shared personnel, management, rolling stock and sales and embalming staff.

The firm in the next town was bought out last year by Service Corporation International (SCI)—the Big Mac of the mortuary trade. They own most of Paris and Australia, a lot of London and

Manhattan. They buy guys like me. They want the brick and mortar, the fifty years of trading on the family name. They want to be like one of the family, mine and yours. At the moment these multinational firms own a fifth of the mortuary dollar volume in the United States. They are in a hurry to own more and more. They go to the state and national conventions of funeral directors' associations. They sponsor swell cocktail parties with open bars and banks of shrimp and Brie, veggies and dip, plenty of hobnob and live entertainment. The air of opulence and available cash is balm to most small-business owners who are accustomed to robbing Peter to pay Paul or holding their own checks to pay the tax man on time. And the state and national associations of funeral directors don't know exactly what to do with them. They like the golf outings and the money being pumped into association events, but are nagged by the sense that they might be sleeping with the enemy. Small businesses need associations, good reputations, the trust of their customers. Big businesses need capital and accountants and lobbyists and synergies. They become, after all, their own associations.

And they need, more than anything, expandable markets. This is where the facts of the marketplace (the more the merrier) and the facts of life (one death and one funeral per customer) run headlong into each other. A new bookstore on every corner will result over time in more books being sold. A Taco Bell at every exit will mean more tacos in the food chain. Lower the price of Cadillacs, and more Cadillacs show up. Movie moguls, politicians, TV preachers, fashion mavens, computer makers—they all know that they can advertise their way into name recognition and increased public appetite for their goods and services. The same is true for Hamburgers and Health Care and Entertainment and Faith.

But a mortuary on every corner will not budge the numbers on the mortality tables. A casket store in every mini-mall will not make the demographics change. Every effort to get folks to die more than once, however convenient we might make it, however good a deal we might offer, however many frequent flyer miles we might promise, has met with fairly general resistance.

Where the market cannot be expanded, as market activity in an unexpandable market increases, the base price of the goods and services must go up. This is why the price of the McBurger and McNovel and McTwoBedroom-Bath-and-a-half-in-the-Suburbs goes *down* as increased volume allows for lower unit price, which increases volume even more, whilst the price of the emerging McFuneral goes *up* to pay for increased costs of acquisitions, advertising and sales in a market where "demand" is stubbornly dismal.

Still, if there's only one death per customer, and though the death rate itself is working its way downward as life expectancy rises and rises—from forty-seven years in 1900 to seventy-six years in 1999—the actuarials on death remain fairly convincing. To wit, everybody's doing it sooner or later. As the demographic aneurysm of seventy-five million baby boomers works its way toward age and decrepitude and death, the future of funeral service (an oddly oxymoronic idiom) looks, well, rosy.

This is why the merger, acquisition and consolidation frenzy has been heavy upon us. If one can't expand the market, the reasoning goes, expand the market share. Create new synergies between supply and distribution and retail outlets. SCI does a deal with Batesville Casket for deep discounts and another with the Catholic church (the original merger-and-acquisition model) for management of its mortuary details through its Christian Funeral

Services (CFS) subsidiary. The church, finding the traffic in souls a little off, reckons the traffic in bodies might do. They read the same demographics as the other multinational conglomerates. Everyone wants to be ready for the bang and whimper of the baby boom, that last hurrah expected between 2010 and 2040 when the annual deaths in the United States will reach 3 million (compared to 2.3 million these days).

A bull market has funded the acquisitions while aggressive preselling puts future market share in the bank.

At the same time, independent funeral directors, frightened that someone will sell the families in their towns something in advance that they have been selling when someone dies, scramble to establish their own pre-need sales programs. They mortgage their brick and mortar to fund telemarketing schemes to fight tele-marketing schemes, junk mail to fend off junk mail, door-to-door solicitors to beat door-to-door solicitors to the punch. Their trade associations, state and federal regulators, famous for nothing so much as doing nothing, do nothing. Their trade press is full of warnings and woe. After a few years of trying to compete locally with a multinational corporation, jumping through the compliance hoops of OSHA and the FTC, and watching the perennial hidden-camera "mortuary-cam" exposés on the network news, more and more second- and third-generation ma-and-pa funeral homes every year sell their good names to the globals, take their cash and stock options and call it a day. Their communities are staked out, stalked, cold-called and "counseled" into transactions with someone they will likely never see again who works for a company with so many layers of corporate cover that accountability gets lost in the logo.

According to the management gurus for the pre-need trade,

folks can't wait to pay for their funerals in advance. But line up any hundred ordinary citizens in a mall, say, or a cathedral or stadium, and ask what they want for their next birthday, and few will say a funeral. The soft market in funeral futures might be connected to the fact that you have to be dead to take delivery. This is why the sell has to be such a hard one. But, ready or not, the transaction with your name and dates on it—the eighteen-gauge Batesville with the changeable hardware, the grave or columbarium space, the Wilbert vault or Eterna Urn, Rock of Ages and perpetual care—is out there looking for you and your Visa or MasterCard.

This is not evil. It is the late-century American Way: to merge and acquire, to buy and sell. The phone companies and churches and automobile companies are doing it. Bigger is better. Global's the rage. And, it is argued, there is nothing inherently wrong with "conglomerate" ownership, nor anything especially noble about "independent" ownership. And, it is true—there are sloppy independent operators and exemplary conglomerate ones.

In practice, however, they are organized around essentially different principles. The publicly traded corporate enterprise is accountable to the international headquarters, the sales quota and the stock holder, while the independent is accountable to the local consumer, including, very often, the local loan officer. The privately owned firm cannot attribute its prices to some distant "home office" or the "district manager." It cannot blame shortfalls in service on "company policy." The privately owned firm must make up in local public trust what it lacks in multinational corporate cover. For independents, market share—present and future—is guaranteed by reputation, while conglomerates place more stock in pre-need sales. Independents count on the name on the sign. Conglomerates count on stock prices and the money in the bank. This is why the hard-sell preselling of funerals has increased in direct proportion to consolidation within funeral service.

The pre*arrangement* of funerals is as old as the pyramids, pre*funding* as old as the money stuffed inside the mattress. But pre*selling*—the junk-mailed, telemarketed briefcase bargain of the memorial counselors and conglomerates—has turned the funeral from an existential event into a retail one. As more package deals are proffered and presold, the public is quite clearly buying less.

Still, it has seemed to many funeral directors that the only choices were to sell hard or to sell out. SCI, along with Loewen (its lately bankrupt Canadian competition) and Stewart Enterprises from Louisiana, have been wildly successful at convincing funeral directors and their associations that the future belonged to them. The bottom-line sensibilities that turn every sadness into a sales-op have convinced a portion of the public that funerals and funeral directors are more trouble than they are worth, and a little like cheeseburgers: all the same.

We are not. The name on my sign, like the names on most, is not Funeral-R-Us or Best Buy Burials or Mortuary Express. The name is mine, my family's, my father and mother's, my brothers' and sisters', our sons' and daughter's. When we serve the families in our town well, they can ignore us by name. When we don't, they can complain by name. It is better consumer protection than the FTC or CNN or anyone in Houston can provide. People talk. Our lives and livelihoods depend on it. The name is worth more than the real estate, the rolling stock or any money in the bank. It is the only one we have. We cannot get another. It determines whom we hire, what we sell, for how much, what we say, who we are and what we do. Home office is here—where the buck stops, where the phone rings in the middle of the night.

THEY ALWAYS CALL in the middle of dinner—these telemarketers. And they're always from places that sound folksy and green —Willow Park, Heritage Creek, Oakland Hills, Forest Lawn. And I'm never quite sure just what they're selling. Is it golf-club memberships or time-share condos or New Age religion or nursing-home care? Maybe they're selling all of the above. "Protection . . . inevitable . . . eventual reality . . ." There's a flurry of meaningful concept words.

Eight times out of ten, between the tossed salad and pizza, it's the cemetery ten miles east off the interstate calling to sell me my "memorial estate." The silky voice reads out the sales pitch involving "millennium discounts" and "first-of-the-century savings" on what she is calling my "final expenses."

I always say I'm a funeral director. I've got my own caskets and vaults and urns—at wholesale. But this doesn't seem to put her off. She's halfway through the first page of script, earnestly inserting my name in the blanks.

"So much better to do this when heads are cool, Mr. Lynch, before the *need* arises. Before your family is vulnerable to someone who might take advantage of their grief. Our counselor will be happy to come to your home!"

This caution is based on the curious and conventional wisdom that the fellow who will cheat you six hours after a death can be trusted six months or six years before you die.

"Preplanning is something you can do for your family. They'll always remember that you cared enough to take care of these difficult decisions. You can be sure everything is done the way you want it."

There's this hint in her voice that my kids won't do me properly—they'll spend too little and blame it on me ("Dad would come back to haunt us if we put him in that casket!"). Or they'll spend too much—wasting the money I wanted spent on my future grandchildren's laptop computers on caskets and sentimentals. Either way they'll never get it right. The fashionable flash of generational mistrust and the basic narcissism of the age are somewhere in the subtext of her soft contralto. That I can run my affairs literally into the ground is a kind of comfort. "Have it your way" she seems to be saying, like Burger King or Frank Sinatra.

My father directed funerals all his life, and whenever we'd ask him what he'd like for himself he'd say only, "You'll know what to do."

We did, of course.

We wept and laughed and waked him, then took him to church, then buried his body in the ground next to our mother, who had died two years before him. We kept their names alive in the talk of their people and kept it on the signs that keep us all accountable to the communities we serve.

"We have many, many options to choose from. Dozens of different payment plans."

She's pushing the right buttons for us boomers now—*planning, choices*. We love these things. Planned parenthood, prenuptials, prearranged funerals—always this hopeful notion that we might prefeel the feelings, the untidy, potentially embarrassing dynamics of birth and love and grief; the blubbering and baby talk, the sense that these unpredictable events might be turned into manageable consumer experiences with numbers and prices that always add up. The notion of "choice" in the contemplation of our own mortality—that part of our nature about which we have no choice—is especially comforting.

"You don't want to be a burden to your children, do you?"

This is the telemarketer's *coup de grâce*, reaching deep into the parental psyche to tap the wellspring of guilt over not taking them to Disney World enough, or to the therapist or the dermatologist, or for never spending enough quality time with them, or for not buying them a pony or a new car or private schools. Here is the chance to make it all up to them by prearranging my own funeral, saving them from all the difficult decisions that they will eventually have to live with.

I see them now—my darling sons, my fierce daughter— heartsore and vulnerable at the news of my untimely and possibly heroic death. I think of them with their cell phones and gold cards and higher educations and inheritance. And it occurs to me: *Why shouldn't I be a burden to my children?*

My children have been a burden to me. Lovely burdens, every one of them. Taking care of their earaches and heartaches and broken bones and disappointments, paying for their colleges and dance classes and car insurance—they've been a burden. I think they were supposed to be. Over the years I've had to explain the death of their grandparents, the suicides of classmates, the divorce of their mother and father, the misbehavior of our political leaders: how love hurts and life isn't fair. I've done car pools and bag lunches and overwhelming questions, broken hearts and Little League and PTA, difficult choices and the facts of life. Sometimes it got really heavy. Sometimes I had to tell them "I don't know."

And bearing these burdens of love and grief has made me feel alive, involved, evolved in ways I never thought I would be; it has made me feel needed and necessary and part of the family. It has made me feel "called" to be a parent. And if it has left me bald and near broke and fairly bewildered, it has likewise left me wondrous, blessed and thankful. After everything, being their father has brought more meaning to my life than any other thing I've ever done or been.

And when I die, bearing the burden of burying me or burning me or blasting me into cyberspace should be theirs to do. My funeral will belong to them and they will be paying for it emotionally, financially, actually. Since they have to live with the decisions, why shouldn't they make them? If I've done my job, then they'll know what to do. If the burden of my death, borne honorably, makes them feel as capable as bearing the sweet burden of their births has made me feel, I can do them the favor of leaving well enough alone.

When I tell the disembodied one on the other end of the line these things, she goes silent. It is not in the script. She hangs up. We return to what's left of our lives and times.

THE FUNERAL IN AMERICA is being reshaped by consolidation and preselling from an intergenerational transaction to a narcissistic one, done according to the wishes of the dead rather than the needs of the living. Instead of serving the living by caring for the dead, it is sold to the living to be cashed in when they are dead. More and more we are mistaking a good deal on a casket for a good funeral, as if a good life-insurance policy was the Good Life.

Whilst death-care moguls and death-care watchdogs work to frame a funeral as only the sum of its parts, numbers that always happily add up—a thing to be marketed like solar heat, sold like insurance or retirement plans and delivered like a bulky home appliance—generations raised with an appetite and aptitude for metaphor, symbol, icon and ceremony will not take leave of their dead without the spiritual, religious and interpersonal comforts of ritual. If life is made easy by technology, it is made meaningful by observance of its rites of passage: the baptisms and marriages and funerals—those rich and deliberate idioms by which we are pronounced alive, in love, gone but not forgotten.

If the men of my generation would not sit out in the waiting room fumbling with cigars waiting for some health-care professional to turn them into fathers; if these men insisted on seeing for themselves, on being there; if these men, in search of meaning, brought us birthing rooms and home births and dads in the delivery room telling their wives to "breathe, honey, breathe . . . ;"and if their wives, the women of my generation, unwilling to have their mothers and fathers die in "intensive care" surrounded by a technology and a parlance that kept the dying distant from the people who "really cared"; if these women brought us hospice and home deaths and the hands-on care of the dying by their own; how long will these men and women sit still while some death-care professional prearranges their parents' disappearance on the cheap? These boomers know the difference between costs and values. They know that a good price on a bad deal is no bargain. They know the difference between fashion and fundamentals. And they will reaffirm their fundamental rights and obligations to witness and care for their dying and their dead.

A funeral is more than the sum of its parts. It has sacred, secular, spiritual, emotional, social and practical duties. A death in the family is not a retail event. It is an existential one.

We occupy a difficult space in the history of obsequies. For many, the traditional religious metaphors have lost their meaning. Likewise ethnic, cultural and geographic communities, undone by diversity, mobility and globalization, have not filled the ceremonial vacuum that exists. In the marketplace, Mitfordized and Wal-Martized, both purveyors and critics have adopted the same limited vocabulary. When more and more of us keep asking what is next, we keep getting more and more detail on what it costs. One group argues that a good funeral costs more. Another argues that a good funeral costs less. Both try to measure the value by the costs. Both mistake the numbers, more or less, for comfort.

If neither the McFuneral nor the McNothing-at-all—however much or little such things cost—meets the needs of those who mourn, maybe we should look for answers elsewhere. If the sad fact of our mortality leaves us desperate for advance planning of casket choices and comprehensive price information, we are alive at the right time, for more than we ever needed to know is available, from the corner mortuary to *caskets.com.* But if the dying of the ones we love and the prospect of our own death leaves us wounded and full of wonder, little in the marketplace will make much sense to us.

The last year of the last century of the last millennium was not a good one for the McFuneral crowd. The Main Street consumer, the Wall Street investor and the mainstream press all seem to be voting in their various ways against globalization in the mortuary trades. Maybe Mission Control shouldn't be in Houston. Maybe the Home Office should be closer to home. The Loewen Group went belly-up, trading at under a dollar, selling what assets it can, at a loss. SCI's stock has fallen from the forties to the single digits in the past year. They blame less flu and Hurricane Floyd among other things. A portfolio of death-care stocks (SRV, STEI, LWN, HB, YRKG) is down more than 70 percent since October 1998. The New York City Department of Consumer Affairs has urged the state's attorney general to prevent further acquisitions by SCI in that city. Lawsuits against SCI have been filed by disgruntled investors, outraged families and Eliza May, the former chief funeral regulator of the state of Texas, who claims she was given her walking papers for investigating SCI on reports of unlicensed personnel embalming bodies. Of course, no one wants to connect the dots between Mrs. May's dismissal and SCI's paying George Bush Sr. $70,000 for a speech to the International Cemetery and Funeral Association or donating $100,000 to his presidential library or helping George Jr. with his political aspirations.

A funeral is not a great investment; it is a sad moment in a family's history. It is not a hedge against inflation; it is a rite of passage. It is not a bargain; it is an effort to make sense of our mortality. It has less to do with actuarial profits and more to do with actual losses. It is not an exercise in salesmanship; it is an exercise in humanity. Both the death-care consumers and the death-care conglomerates ignore such distinctions at their peril.

PERHAPS IF POETS phoned in the middle of dinner, to sell us dactyls and pentameters instead of caskets or cremation deals—perhaps death and remembrance would be more meaningful. Perhaps this life's mysteries are better served by metaphor than marketing schemes. For the unspeakable sadnesses and their related joys, a good poem, like a good funeral, makes the most sense when we need it most. Maybe something by Conrad Hilberry, or something from William Carlos Williams, the late good doctor who wrote in "Tract" "I will teach you my townspeople / how to perform a funeral"—or something by Michael Heffernan, say, from whose sestina called "Famous Last Words" these yet-to-be-famous last words are taken:

> *Sometimes I have to laugh: the more you wait,*
> *the more you end up wishing you could up*
> *and have a look at what will happen next.*
> *Where did it ever get you, from the start,*
> *the time or two you said you'd wait and see,*
> *when all you really wanted was to drink*
>
> *it all in, all of it, in one long drink*
> *that would relieve you of the need to wait*
> *for the Right Moment? A man's time is up*
> *too soon in this quick world. As for the next,*
> *I think I have a theory: first you start*
> *to notice how you can't move, think or see . . .*

Not long after which, by all accounts, we die.

Johnny, We Hardly Knew You

L ondon, a city well known for its tasteful understatement, particularly in emotive fashions, pulled out all the stops that summer when Princess Diana died. Her funeral was by all accounts the single most public event in history, broadcast around the globe in living color and boldfaced type. There was open grief, some genuine, some suspect; there was perhaps some guilt, some shame, maybe, in some quarters, even some relief. There was a week-long planetary wake during which responses ranged from foolish to honorable, brave to heartbreaking, maddening to memorable. There were acres of flowers, the singing of sad songs, quickly drafted elegies in the daily papers. There was a body, processed through town, taken into church, borne home at last for burial. Real sons, real siblings, unwelcome realities in brutal abundance.

Like all things that happen in real time, it left room for the ridiculous and the sublime and most things in between. But in the end, it seemed to work. It was a "good" funeral. It got the dead and the living where they needed to go, even if they had to duck the cameras and dodge the microphones on their way.

Of course, now the locals have begun to wonder if maybe it wasn't all a little "over the top." There's some worry among churchmen over the Cult of Diana, rumors that she isn't buried at Althorp at all, the inevitable conspiracy theories. There are new university courses in Dianaology, nearly a million new Web sites in her name, fights over money in the memorial fund. There's gold in the Diana Memorial Hills and everyone seems intent on mining some. So clearly, the English have good reason to wonder.

So have we all.

Taking a lesson from the royals' experience, the Kennedys of D.C., Manhattan and Hyannis, long willing to bear the costs of public life, seem no longer willing to share their private griefs with a media so driven by ratings and the need to fill airtime that nothing is off limits anymore.

They are right to be wary.

When John Kennedy, Jr., his wife and her sister died too soon last summer, their family met the boat that brought their bodies to shore. Their people accompanied the bodies to the Duxbury crematory on Cape Cod, where, through the night, the bodies were burned. Then they took the ashes out to sea and let them go. Then they went to church, where real family and real friends were gathered. In consideration of the empathies of their countrymen, copies of eulogies and statements of gratitude were released to the press. Then they returned to the life with its losses.

Of course, the news of it, the story, the facts of the matter, are terribly brief and profoundly sad. And sadness is known to everyone, so we ordinary citizens, members of the one species, are likely to pause or pray or make some signal of our fellow feeling. But every sadness does not belong to everyone.

At least it didn't until very lately.

Though the sum and substance of just what happened could be reported worldwide in a matter of minutes and paragraphs, the media's appetite for filler and content requires that more than just the news be reported. By dressing public interest and morbid curiosity in the needful garb of bereavement, they have become our virtual grief therapists, trumping the squad of "facilitators" that the president apparently keeps at the ready to dispatch to Oklahoma City or Littleton or wherever the next "need" arises. The anchorpersons and talking heads dress in dark clothes, voices are toned down to the occasion, a title and a logo are assigned to it all, theme music heavy on violins is added, experts from anywhere hold forth, anyone who knew anyone who knew anyone is interviewed, never-before-seen video clips appear, and appear again, and again, and again and again. The ubiquitous "makeshift shrine" and "spontaneous memorial" will materialize, from which updates are broadcast on the quarter hour, and citizens who felt they had to *do* something gab for the cameras and go their ways. Close-up on the tear-jerking note attached to a teddy bear or roses or balloons. Weeks later the memorial video can be had by calling a toll-free number with one's credit card handy. The glossy mags print commemorative issues.

Tragedy-cam and Grief TV give couch potatoes easy access to the "therapies" of "national mourning" for people they have no acquaintance with or knowledge of or interest in except as covers on the magazines in waiting rooms and checkout lines. With round-the-clock coverage on three cable channels and network news magazines and special reports, no one need change their schedule, put on a suit, order flowers, bake a casserole, go to the funeral home or church, try to find something of comfort to say or endure the difficult quiet of genuine grief when words fail, when nothing can be said. Nor need they see a body or help carry one or pay for anything, or perpetually care. They needn't budge. The catharsis is user-friendly, the "healing" home delivered. "Being there" for perfect strangers has never been easier. When they've had enough they can grab a DoveBar, flick to The Movie Channel or the Home Shopping Network and wait until the helicopters locate another outrage to zoom in on.

Whatever they have experienced, it is not grief. Grief is the tax we pay on our attachments, not on our interests or diversions or entertainments. We grieve in keeping with the table stakes of our relationships, according to the emotional capital we invest in the lives and times of others, that portion of ourselves we ante up before the cards are dealt. We might be curious about our losses when we play to kill time, or interested when we play for fun, or even obsessed a little if we find the game compelling. But we grieve for losses only in games we play for keeps—real love, real hate, real attachments broken.

And what the networks offer us is the therapy of spectacle, excess and sedation—our humanity dulled by megadoses, like too much pornography dulls real sex, too much volume eventually deafens, and too much information dulls the truth.

IS THE IMPULSE TO MAXIMIZE our responses to the deaths of icons and celebrities a compensation for the tendency to minimize our responses to the deaths that ought to really matter— those of our own people? Might some of the flowers dumped at Kensington Palace or TriBeCa have been better sent in sympathy or memory of real neighbors and friends? Did some of those tears shed these past summers belong to the parents or spouses or children whose deaths were never witnessed, ritualized or grieved enough long years before? Do we compensate for local understatement by global hyperbole?

Perhaps if we were more willing to leave ourselves open to grief—deregulated, unplanned, unruly, potentially embarrassing grief—and bear its burdens honorably, we'd have less free-floating, unattached heartache to spend on the increasingly "packaged" bereavement-ops the media serves up. Maybe if we were better at wakes and funerals, those ancient parlor games we used to play for keeps, by which we buried or burned our own dead more publicly and mourned our local losses openly, we could turn off the TVs. We could let our celebrities rest in peace.

Y2Kat

B y the time you read this the cat will be dead.

So long have I longed for the truth of that utterance that I have grown mad-anxious with the longing for it. But the sweet odor of truth is in it now, oozing from the little pores of the sentence like frankincense. *By the time you read this the cat will be dead.* Can you smell the truth and beauty of it there?

Though the cat is not presently dead, here in the exact moment of these contemplations, in the coincidence of my writing such matters down, consigning the details of my dark hopes to a text, as it were; nonetheless, by the time you read this the fact will have bloomed, fully fledged in the corpse of a cat who will be dead, as I said, by the time you read this. It has been, as final, finished details always are, cut in stone.

About which more, alas, anon.

For now let me say, simply and for the record, that I've hated the cat. And that I hate the cat. Furthermore, I am, at this very moment, hating the cat and tomorrow will be hating the cat some more. There is no tense or participle or variation of the verb *to hate* that does not apply to my relations with the cat.

By this time next week I will have been hating the cat for all but a few months of all but a few years of the last two decades of the last century of the second millennium. It is the only century my dear dead parents lived in, the only one that several loyal dogs of my acquaintance took breath from, the only millennium that Joyce or Yeats or Edna St. Vincent Millay were alive in. Ted Hughes did not outlive it or Frank Sinatra or Mother Teresa. They're all dead. John Lennon, Roy Rogers, Roy Orbison, Princess Di. Remembered quite rightly but nonetheless dead.

And the cat, as I write this, is still alive? Is there no one else out there to share my outrage? That a much-despised gray angora should occupy two millennia whilst Mohandas Gandhi and Martin Luther King, Jr. only one? Either way, if, by the grace of God and the luck of the actuarial draw, I am allowed to draw breath in the new millennium, to be, as it were, a citizen of the Old Age and the New One, I have made it my duty to vouchsafe the cat does not. It is the least I can do—a self-imposed debt to history and the future. You can take it to the bank, bet the ranch, let it ride—if I'm alive for a few more months, by the time you read this the cat will be dead.

SOME FELLOW WITH TOO MUCH TIME on his hands once opined that the world is divided into those who hate cats and those who love them. Would that things were just so simple. We could quit the Balkans and Belfast and other border wars. All the imbroglios of distrust and distemper that infect the planet could be flushed into history if all that divided the species were cats. But let me say from the get-go that my hatred for the cat is not so simple as that. It is not the *feline* in general but this cat in particular that I hate (have hated, am hating, will hate, etc.). That it is a cat is only incidental to the fact that it is hateful. The ability of our species to abhor particular members of a subspecies whilst otherwise approving of the sort at large is well established. The point is also worth making that my hatred for the cat is in no way tied to species elitism, or animal harassment, or any all-encompassing prejudice against four-legged sorts. Nothing like that. Why, only last month (and I have witnesses), whilst visiting my cottage in West Clare, I was caught frying rashers and black pudding for a stray cat that visited every morning during our stay there. I set out fresh bacon and fresh milk and a bit of cheese and, in the evenings, a bit of fresh mackerel from the several dozen of same I'd liberate from the sea every day, as is my habit and custom there. I even began to call the cat by little familiar gender-indifferent names the way my late cousin Nora, from whom I'd inherited the house, was known to call her mousers. "Tippins" and "Blackie" and "Pookie" and such noises as that, because a hungry cat around a country house is no bad thing, especially near the changing of seasons, when the local rodentia are enthused about establishing cushy quarters behind the old cooker and fridge and in the press, where the back boiler keeps the bedclothes and linens warm.

So it can be said outright that I approve of the feline in the larger sense and only hate this one fat, old, lazy, gray she-cat; this one and only good-for-nothing beast that has, for lo! these past two decades now, refused to call it quits of my house. It will not die or run away or get lost like any normal cat would do.

Which is why I hate *this* cat. Though my hating of this cat neither increases nor decreases the statistical likelihood of my hating another cat, or loving another cat. My hatred for this cat in particular is unrelated to my associations, whatever they may be, with cats in general.

And maybe I belabor this point, but I want it on the record once and for all that I don't hate cats. I want the record clear on this because once I wrote a passionately unflattering poem about a former spouse, the mother of my children, in the months that followed our divorce years ago. However well crafted, this malediction, which appeared in my first slim volume of poems, was the reason for a damning little comment from at least one reviewer to the effect that "Mr. Lynch apparently does not like women."

Nothing, I want the record to show, could be further from the truth. Must one's distemper with one woman mark him or her ever as a Woman Hater? Remember the cat we are after talking about?

THE SPIRIT OF THE THING was, to be sure, unfortunate. These were bad old times for all of us.

There I was, dumped in my mid-thirties when my wife fell in love with a man from her video-production class at the community college. It is, I suppose, fair to say that before falling in love with him she fell out of love with me, with the idea of being the wife and homemaker—two thankless jobs, then as now—with the whole *Leave It to Beaver,* Love Conquers All, early Joni Mitchell vision of things that had brought us together twelve years before. Gone were the dreams of suburban bliss, secure income, a family and a social life. Gone were the satisfactions of safe and certain, albeit predictable, sex.

She wanted something "more."

There'd been signs I'd chosen mostly to ignore, distracting myself with work and writing, playing with the kids, while she seemed to be growing distant from us. She flew east to visit a woman friend and ended up in the island home of an older man she'd had a crush on as a girl. There were more trips east. Phone bills inflated. Afraid of the answers, I didn't ask questions. By the time the fellow from the community college started calling, I was really the last to know.

In the parsing of intimacies fashionable then, she loved me but was no longer, and furthermore maybe never really had been, *in love* with me. It was all a mistake she'd rushed into, she was sorry. She really didn't want to hurt me, but I was like a weight around her neck dragging her down, keeping her from realizing her full potential. There was talk of "spreading her wings," and she really reckoned she had just "outgrown" me and the marriage. It sounded like the cover copy on *Cosmopolitan.* I said I thought for the sake of the children we ought to seek counseling, what with four little lives hanging in the balance.

We found a husband-and-wife team in the university town nearby. They'd written a book and came highly recommended. There were personality assessments and lots of multiple-choice tests. We had a few joint sessions that mostly ended with her stomping out. "Sabotage," the shrinks called it. We persevered. It wasn't that I'd done anything wrong, it was just that I was fairly boring. I paid the bills, helped with the kids, was sexually attentive, but too routine. I didn't hit or scream or bully or sleep around. Neither did I excite or inspire or make her weak with desire the way the fellow from the community college did. She was spending more and more time on the phone, out late with "friends," ever busy with "lab projects" at school.

We divided into individual sessions. She talked with the wife. I talked with the husband. We did more questionnaires. He told me that she was already "psychologically divorced" and that I shouldn't hold out much hope for repair. He told me that there were women out there who would give anything for the kind of love and loyalty I offered. I didn't believe him. I felt like shit.

There's this memory I have of working on a sonnet while she sat at the table in the next room cursing at an overdraft notice from the bank. She'd established a separate checking account so that what was mine was ours and what was hers was hers. Hers was apparently overdrawn. She was badmouthing the checkbook and punching the calculator and seemed to be trying to tell me something. She was sometimes violent with animate and inanimate things.

"If you want help with that, all you need do is ask me," I said.

Weeks with the shrink had taught me to talk like this.

"It's all here if you want to help," she said.

I said that I didn't really want to help. I had the checkbook at the office and the checkbook for the Rotary Club and the checkbook of our household accounts to keep balanced, so that I really didn't want or need another set of books to juggle.

"But if you want help," I told her, "all you have to say is, 'Please, help me,' and, of course, I will."

"Okay, fine, then, please," she said, and I went to take a look.

She had added something instead of subtracting. The miscalculation amounted to seventy-five dollars and overdraft fees. When I pointed this out to her she looked at me with cool contempt. I had found the problem. Now what was I going to do about it? What was clear to me then was that if I bailed her out, if I gave her the money, I'd be the asshole who did. If I didn't, then I'd be the asshole who didn't. Either way I was going to be the asshole.

By midsummer things had gone from bad to worse. We

agreed to go on a long-planned family vacation. We'd paid the deposit and reserved the cottage on the lake the year before, when we'd been happy there. Bad as things were, I still held out hope.

One night, after the kids had gone to bed all sunburned and ignorant of what was looming, I told her that her relationship with her "friend" really hurt me, that it was making me crazy, and that if we were going to work on the marriage, at the least we should not confuse matters with other liaisons. I told her that I could abide playing the cuckold but I couldn't abide having to play the fool as well.

When she left the next afternoon after preening all morning, ready and willing and perfumed, I knew she had arranged to meet her lover. I sat on a log on the beach with the children, watching the lake and knowing it was finished. I got a sinker from my tackle box and, with a bit of shoelace, fashioned it into a kind of necklace. When she returned from her assignation, I asked her to walk with me down the beach. I gave her the little necklace and said she'd convinced me. I told her that I would think of our marriage as dead and always think of us in the past tense and that I'd never weigh her down again. The next day we assembled the children in the cottage and told them all the ordinary lies failed marrieds must tell the ones they've failed the most—how everything was going to be all right and that even though Mommy and Daddy didn't love each other anymore we both loved them more than anything in the world and how it wasn't "about" them, and everything would be all right, and they wouldn't have to move and of course Mommy and Daddy still "liked" each other and everything would be all right.

They were ten, nine, six and four when it happened. The day sits like a lump of coal in their lives, sometimes smoldering, sometimes dark and cool, but always there, always ready to be reddened by forces still out of our control.

In the end, after the lawyers and shrinks, after all the hateful ballyhoo of tearing sheets, after all the sadness and the sundering, I borrowed enough to write her a check for her half of the much-mortgaged "marital home." She left with her clothes, half the furnishings, high hopes for a new life, the cash, the cat and her visitation rights.

"Good riddance" is the thing I said.

I found myself the court-awarded custodial parent of four minor children, crazy with bag lunches and laundry, feeling the failure, seething quietly at the cruel twists of fate.

Poetry is not therapy. Got a problem? I say call a priest, see a shrink, have at one of those 900 numbers, take up macramé or marathons. But don't, for God's sake, think that you can write yourself into or out of good mental hygiene. It's not going to happen. Trust me on this.

So I called the priest. He brought by forms for an annulment. He said I was a young man and would want to marry again and this would allow me to do it in church. All that was required was a fairly comprehensive history of my former wife's business and my own. When I told him I wouldn't be sending the intimate details of my failed married life downtown to the chancery for a panel of celibates to "consider," he warned that without an annulment I could get only a "civil" marriage if I ever wed again. I said I thought that would be an improvement on the last one. I couldn't imagine being married again.

As for shrinks, I'm afraid I had lost my faith. Oh, I was taking the kids, once a week. And it was good for them. But the bills were getting prohibitive and I really didn't want to "get in touch with my feelings." That was an altogether frightening prospect. A large dose of Irish every night kept me a safe distance from myself and helped me sleep and kept my anger keen.

I don't run or do crafts, the more's the pity.

And that's how the unfortunate poem came to be.

"For the Ex-Wife on the Occasion of Her Birthday" gave voice to my unspeakable rage—a rage that simmered for a year before finding its way into carefully crafted lines, seventy or so of them—a kind of bitter litany, in loose blank verse, of all the things I claimed *not* to wish on her, venom done up as carefully off-rhymed birthday greetings, to wit:

> . . . *tumors or loose stools*
> *blood in your urine, oozing from any orifice*
> *the list is endless of those ills I do not pray befall you.*
> *Night sweats, occasional itching, PMS,*
> *fits, starts, ticks, boils, bad vibes, vaginal odors,*
> *emotional upheavals or hormonal disorders;*
> *green discharges, lumps, growths, nor tell-tale signs of gray;*
> *dry heaves, hiccups, heartbreaks, fallen ovaries*
> *nor cramps—before, during or after. I pray you only*
> *laughter in the face of your mortality . . .*

There was more, of course. Plenty more: mention of her mother, her "donkey lovers," her "whining discontent" and "all those hapless duties husbanding a woman of [her] disenchant-ments came to be." It finished with an allusion to the ancient Irish epic about Mad Sweeney, who was cursed into a bird and made "to nest among the mounds of dung" back in the good old days when "all that ever came with age was wisdom." It was abusive, excessive, full of the half-rhymes and whole truths that make poems memorable.

The first time I aired it at a reading, some men cheered, some women hissed, but mostly everyone roared with laughter. The feel of the words in my mouth was a kind of balm. It made me feel better than any therapy. And though poetry is not therapy, every time I read it I felt better and better. Because every time I read it I felt more in control of a life that was still spinning out of control, with drink and house duties and a business to run and the lives of my children in constant danger. I feared my anger and I feared its opposite.

Once, with my darling daughter in earshot, I was coaxed into reading it to a group of writers at a summer workshop in northern Michigan. It had earned a certain celebrity by now. To my everlasting shame, I never thought how much hearing it would hurt her. And by the time I saw the pain and confusion in her face, I was too far into it to turn around. Or I was having too good a time being the center of attention. Later, I tried to tell her that the poem was really not *about* her mother, but *about* my anger, and that as a poet, I had artistic rights and license in the matter, that I was entitled to my feelings and their free expression. To her credit she did not believe me.

Once, at the University of Cincinnati, the poet and critic Richard Howard did me the honor of attending a reading of mine. At the end he was all praise, mentioning this poem and that poem, quoting me to me. It was an honor to have the great man saying such things. Then he said, "The poem for the ex-wife is really remarkable. You should probably never read it again."

It was hard to make out what it was he meant. Was he trying

to save me from the PC police that patrolled the universities? Or was he trying to save me from my own dark habits, which he recognized this poem was an emblem of?

It was strange counsel from a wise man and I took it. I've never read the poem to an audience since. The book is now out of print. The few thousand copies it sold are mostly in libraries or used-book stores now. The poem has never been anthologized. It and the rage it gave voice to are gone.

NOT LONG THEREAFTER I began hating the cat.

SOME POP-PSYCHERS are maybe saying now, sure, the cat and the ex-wife are in some way connected. Maybe you're throwing around words like *transference* or *surrogate* or *scapegoat* or such. The dear knows I wish they *were* connected. The truth is they deserve each other. I was pleased when the one left with the other.

At the time I did not hate the cat. I could have gone either way on the thing. Still, I figured my hands were full enough of living, breathing things to care for. Every other weekend she would take the kids, some Tuesdays, some Thursdays, depending on her schedule. The exercise of her visitation rights was always "optional," "contingent," "flexible," ever subject to the frequently shifting realities of her life and times. New housing, new romance, new jobs, new deals—the multiple variables made for a variable schedule. No plans could be made because nothing was certain. We would sit waiting in a kind of expectant limbo, for "Saturday at noon" or "Thursday by dinnertime"—the kids kept from straying too far from the yard, in case she'd come. Then the call would come—she was running a little late—twenty minutes, two hours, a day, a week. Or there'd be "rain checks" or "makeups" or "tomorrow, for sure." It was years before we learned not to work our lives around her ever-changing schedule.

So in the early going I counted as a comfort that, though the children and the dog and the mortgage were my daily duties, the cat was hers, and a good riddance to it. I did not hate the cat then. I had no cause to.

For reasons best known to my former spouse, not six months after she'd moved out with the cat, back it came with its bowl and box of Tender Vittles and pan full of used kitty litter. It seems it was not working out with the new lifestyle or living space.

This pleased the children, especially my middle son, who's fondness for the cat owed, I supposed, to the sweetness in him, his gentle habits and the fact that he and the cat were about the same age—both of them going on seven that year. His brothers and sister, to be sure, all fed the thing and let it in and out the door and ranged between endearments and indifference in their dealings with it, but Michael's attachment to the cat seemed primal. They understood each other's eyes and sounds and moods and needs.

Because I loved the boy I could abide the cat's return. Whilst marketing I'd find my way to the pet-foods aisle for little tinned delicacies, bags of kitty litter, even those little pastel-colored fishy-scented treats with which to curry the cat's favor. At a church rummage sale I paid good money for one of those cushy little oval-shaped affairs in which the cat never learned to sleep next to Mike's bed, preferring, instead, to curl itself in the corner by the pillow on which my darling golden boy himself would slumber.

I even tried to pet it once. It rose and walked out of the room, sneezing as it went, as if it were allergic to me. Its indifference I could tolerate. All cats—it is well known—can take or leave their humans. But the cat seemed to bear toward me a malice quite inexplicable considering that I housed it, fed it, paid for its vaccinations and grooming, observed the little regimens to prevent distemper, diarrhea, hangnails and heartworms. It not only was disinterested in my life, it seemed disturbed by my very being. Whatever I'd do, enough was never enough. Whatever I didn't do, it was too much. Damned if I did or if I didn't—the cat's discontent, at least so far as I was concerned, was manifest. It was developing an "attitude" with me. While it was always a bother, it could not, itself, be bothered to catch a mouse, or provide good company. Only Mike could make it purr.

Those few moments in the day not devoted to the office or the menu or the wash-and-wear or livery services, those minutes in which I reserved the right to hear my own self think, were always being interrupted by the cat. It whined, it roared, it needed to go out, come in, be fed or watered or left alone.

I'd get the children bathed, their homework done. I read to them. We'd say their little bedtime prayers and then I'd sneak downstairs to the day's remains—the sink full of dishes, the bathtub ring, the sad facts of the matter. I'd pour whiskey in a glass, assemble myself at my writing desk and take up revisions to a poem, sent back by some "important" literary journal that paid nothing and was read by no one, whose editor hadn't bothered beyond a form-letter version of the same rejection I saw in every aspect of my life. I'd be laboring over some adjective, some verb, some salvation from the word-horde that would make the thing desirable, when the cat would come roaring its late-night hunger or desires. It would not eat unless I watched it eat. It would not leave unless I held the door. In all weathers it would take its time coming and going. Still, for all my efforts, it looked upon me as a necessary evil. Thus were the seeds of my dislike of it sown.

Worse still were the rare nights when the children would be away with their mother. Sometimes a woman friend would spend the night. I'd freshen the bed linens, tidy everything, put the music on and put the cat outdoors. I remember one late December in particular. The children were spending Christmas with their mom. My true love and I had opened our gifts, built a fire, watched old movies on the TV and made our way upstairs, intent on hours of blessed coupling and uncoupling. It was bitter outside, the wind was howling, the snow drifting up and down the darkened streets, and the warmth of our consortium seemed so much more the gift. We were touching each other in that way that lovers do—slowly, deliberate, willing to pleasure the other for one's own pleasure's sake. The candles, the music, the beauty of her body, the quiet in the house—it almost seemed as if I wasn't trapped and desperate and utterly rejected; it almost seemed as if I would survive.

It was then that I heard the cat outside the bedroom window. I had put it outside in hopes that it would freeze. At first it only meowed. Then it whined, the sound of it driven on the cold wind through the old walls of the house. Then it began to roar. Then it began to scratch at the corner of the window sash. The mood was being broken badly. I rose from our reveries, opened the curtains and saw the evil green eyes looking back at me. It had, apparently, made its way up the magnolia tree I'd planted too near the house some years before—a Valentine's Day gift to the former missus— and onto the little roof outside my bedroom window from whence it sat making known its objections to our privacy and purpose. I opened the window and tried to knock it off the roof with a shoe, but it was too sure-footed. Then I thought I'd coax it in from the cold and that would satisfy it. It approached the open window but would not come in. It roared the louder. My shins were freezing, my passions were shriveling. It paced up and back the roof. The wind and snow were chilling the interior. It would neither come nor go. Not until I lumbered downstairs, naked and cursing, and opened the side door by the bald magnolia and called out the gray cat's name did it deign to come down the magnolia tree, across the snowdrift, up the steps and into the house. By the time I got back upstairs, the room was freezing, the woman sleeping, the candles quenched, the music quieted. I went downstairs to kill the cat with a blunt object but couldn't find it, though I searched for hours, shaking the box full of kitty treats, holding the baseball bat aloft, my eyes wild with murder and mayhem in them.

TO LOATHE SOMETHING your child loves is difficult. To harbor far-from-kindly feelings toward the object of an innocent's affection is cause for secrecy. You cannot speak of the damage you would like to do it for fear of damaging the youngster. Every divorced parent knows these things. To let some loose word slip about one's former spouse's deplorable habits in earshot of the child is bad form. Already divided by divorce, the little self is cleft again by the war of words that puts the heart at odds with its own affections and identity. To object is a betrayal. To agree is a betrayal too. To consent, by silence, festers in the heart.

And knowing this I did my best around the children, to say only positive things about their mother, how she loved them dearly and would always be "there" for them, though where "there" was was often anyone's guess. And failing that, to say nothing at all. And when my hateful poem hurt them all, when it was published in a book for all to see, I resolved never to write about their mother again, or my righteous anger, or my rage.

In my head I knew that what was good for her was good for our children. Her sanity, her security, her safety, her happiness— her well-being inured to the well-being of my sons and daughter. So while a part of me wished for her disappearance from our lives, I adopted, as a form of spiritual exercise, the habit of genuine daily prayer on her behalf.

And praying for the ones that piss you off can make for miracles. Whatever was going on in her life, mine got some better.

I quit drinking. The anger subsided.

I quit writing for fear it might rekindle the rage.

I quit fighting with my former spouse. I quit talking to her altogether.

The sound of a voice I recognized as my own—reason and rhyming and ranting—grew still. I listened for a while. But it was gone.

The children grew in grace and in beauty.

I might've held my peace but for the cat.

BY FORTY I had chest pains and teenagers, a new woman in my life, money in the bank and a cat that was trying to kill me.

My abhorrence of the thing, despite every effort to keep it corked, was beginning to leak into my daily meditations. Behind the glad face I turned toward my sons and daughter in the conduct of my parental duties was the certainty of the malice she bore me, the sense I had of her inherent evil and the worry over the powers she might have. One night she woke me from a deep sleep with her fierce crying. Making my way downstairs to fix what ailed her, I nearly fell to my death at the diabolical sound she made when I stepped on her tail. She had positioned herself halfway up the staircase in the dark, awakened me with her roaring and plotted the fatal fall or infarction to finish me. Only deft footwork and good conditioning saved me that night. I chased the thing around with a hammer in preemptive self-defense but could not catch her. Awakened by the ruckus, Michael came down half-asleep, took her up in his arms and, speaking baby talk to her—"Whazamatter, kiddy? Did that old man wake you up?"—took her up to bed. I stood barefooted on the cold kitchen floor, clenching a hammer, blazing with adrenaline and revulsion. I did not sleep for days.

As they aged, their attachment only grew stronger. He could not see the fiend beneath the fur. He'd rub her and brush her, and speak to her in the voice one saves for one's beloved. He told me once, if she should ever die, he wanted to have her taxidermied. Some mornings I'd say she was looking especially lovely and we could have her stuffed today, thus freezing in time her abundant "beauty," and I would pay for the procedure. Mike wasn't amused. My detestation festered. My heart hurt with it, my head ached with it, my bowel burned with it. Because I could not speak my rage, it spoke to me.

AMONG THE GIFTS I got one Christmas was a vocabulary calendar. Every day of the new year brought a new word to be learned and used and incorporated into the common speech. Along with the news that it was Wednesday 30 June 1990 came *phlegm*: "\flem\ n 1: thick mucus secreted in abnormal quantity *2a: dull apathetic coldness or indifference b: intrepid coolness or calm fortitude." And, of course, it would be used in a sentence: "°Burt surveyed the accident scene with a lofty phlegm, maintaining the controlled detachment that allowed him to report on such grim events." Better still, on the back of the page was some little-known etymological detail with which you might amaze your friends over dinner, if you had any.

> The ancient Greek physician Hippocrates theorized that human personalities were controlled by four humors: blood (dominant in cheerful, optimistic types), black bile (which rendered a soul gloomy and melancholy), yellow bile (the source of irritable, angry attitudes) and phlegm (ruling cool, unemotional types). Logically, when the Greeks related these humors to their four elements (air, earth, fire and water), phlegm was linked to water. But the word's etymology defies logic: "phlegm" traces back to the Greek verb *phlegein*, which means "to burn."

Oh, how I longed to be like Burt, to exude detachment, to be free of the black bile, rid of the yellow bile, returned to my ordinarily optimistic blood, to achieve "intrepid coolness" and "calm fortitude"; to be the third-person singular masculine subject of a sentence my friends would use in which not too long after the appropriate verb the predicate object would be *phlegm*.

Such was the condition of my life that a new word every day seemed a beatitude, holding forth a bouquet of promise and possibilities.

Some day in May you'd get *ennui*. You'd use it ten times before dinner and folks would say, "My, but he's enjoying the calendar this year." Later there'd be *irrefragable* and *mugwump* and, in November, *penultimate*.

It was in March, a gray day I remember, near the vernal equinox, I first encountered the word *grimalkin*: "\gri-`mo(l)-ken\n: a domestic cat; especially: an old female cat." The use in a sentence was unremarkable, but the bit of detail on the back was this:

In the opening scene of *Macbeth*, one of the three witches planning to meet with Macbeth announces, "I come, Graymalkin!" Shakespeare's "graymalkin" literally meant "gray cat" and figuratively referred to the familiar, or spirit servant, of the witch. The "gray" in "graymalkin" is, of course, the color; the "malkin" was a nickname for Mary, Matilda, or Maude that came to be used in dialect as a general name for a cat (or other animal) or an untidy woman. By the 1630s, "graymalkin" had been altered to the modern spelling "grimalkin."

I am a slave to words. I am their servant. The acoustics and meanings, their sounds and sense, sometimes make me shiver— the precision, the liberties, the health and healing in their meanings. Language is the first among God's many gifts. To name and proclaim makes us feel like gods. To define and discern, to clarify and articulate, to affirm—surely this was what our maker had in mind when we were made in that image and likeness. Not the beard or lightning bolts or bluster. It was no big bang. It was a whisper. It was a word made flesh—our Creation. And the real power of Creation is the power of words to guard us like angels, to protect and defend and define us; to incite, and excite, and inspire; to separate us from the grunting, growling, noisome, wordless, worthless meowing things. Thus when I came upon this word *gri-malkin*—this "gray cat," this "familiar of a witch," this "untidy woman"—I saw it as the gift of my personal savior. Not, mind you, the accidental kindness of a random god. No, this was a word with my name on it, sent from a heaven where my name was known, by a God who knew the hairs on my head the way the First Baptists have always claimed He (for they think of him as a He) did. By a God who said to Himself, that poor crazy hopeless case down there doesn't need a good word, he needs this good word: *grimalkin*.

I sat at my desk with a blank sheet of paper, filled my best pen with fresh black ink and in my best hand wrote at the top of the page, *GRIMALKIN*.

As all good words do, it incited such a riot in my brainy parts that bits of verse began to spark all over. Of a sudden the world took on a clarity and reason. Everything in Creation began to hum with the sense of it. The divisions in my psyche were made as one. I was speaking in dactyls and iambs and trochees. Things began almost to rhyme. The acoustics of even the most humdrum words took on the vaulted, echoey tone of prayer and incantation. I began at once to write it down.

The cat was working its way across the living room carpet, crying out its customary discontent, strutting the well-known facts of the matter that because I loved the boy who loved her, I had to abide its miseries, its contemptuous green eyes fixed on me with long-established indifference. The first line came to me immediately:

One of these days she will lie there and be dead.

How had this profound comfort kept itself from me these long, silent years? All I had to do was outlive the thing. How long can a cat live, I asked myself? Nothing that miserable can enjoy a long life—the black bile, the yellow bile, would certainly kill it. And then?

> *I'll take her out back in a garbage bag*
> *and bury her among my son's canaries*

Oh, happy thought! Oh, blessed harbingings!

> *the ill-fated turtles, a pair of angel fish,*
> *the tragic and mannerly household pests*
> *that had the better sense to take their leaves*
> *before their welcomes or my patience had worn thin.*

Michael came in for lemonade and, seeing the strange glee in my eyes, asked, "What are you writing, Dad?"

"A poem about your cat."

"Deep down inside you really love her, don't you, Dad?"

I said nothing.

"Be sure and put my name in it." Mike was jealous of his sister, whose name appeared in the title of my first collection.

> *For twelve long years I've suffered this damn cat.*
> *While Mike, my darling middle son, himself*
> *twelve years this coming May, has grown into*
> *the tender, if quick-tempered manchild*
> *his breeding blessed and cursed him to become.*
> *And only his affection keeps the cat alive*

It was true. Michael, like his brothers and sister, was the making of his mother and his father, blessed and cursed by both of us with talents and tendencies, gifts from God, each one of them. And like all things made by God and humankind, a combination of love and rage, beauty and beastliness and benignity.

> *though more than once I've threatened violence:*
> *the brick and burlap in the river recompense*
> *for mounds of furballs littering the house*
> *choking the vacuum cleaner, or what's worse*
> *shit in the closets, piss in the planters, mice*
> *that winter indoors safely as she sleeps*
> *curled about a table-leg, vigilant*
> *as any knick-knack in a partial coma.*

I hated the cat. And I had good reasons. And saying them out loud, writing them down, giving them voice, made them sound convincing.

> *But Mike, of course, is blind to all of it—*
> *the gray angora breed of arrogance,*
> *the sluttish roar, the way she disappears for days*
> *sex desperate, once or twice a year,*
> *urgently ripping her way out the screen door*
> *to have her way with everything that moves*
> *while Mike sits up with tuna fish and worry,*
> *crying into the darkness, "Here kitty kitty"*
> *mindless of her whorish treacheries*
> *or of her crimes against upholsteries—*

I loved that rhyme, *treacheries, upholsteries.* Such gifts were signs that God was on my side. I wrote as if I had a mission, as if I were the channel of Creation and the Truth.

> *the sofas, loveseats, wingbacks, easy chairs*
> *she's puked and mauled into dilapidation.*

I have this reoccurring dream of driving her
deep into the desert east of town
and dumping her out there with a few days' feed
and water. In the dream, she's always found
by kindly tribespeople who eat her kind
on certain holydays as a form of penance.

Mike came in asking for lunch, but, seeing in my eyes the dull glaze of creation, decided, wisely, not to press the matter. He took up his cat, who looked at me with its own feckless wisdom, and both of them went back outdoors.

God knows, I don't know what he sees in her.
Sometimes he holds her like a child in his arms
rubbing her underside until she sounds
like one of those battery powered vibrators
folks claim to use for the ache in their shoulders.
And under Mike's protection she will fix
her indolent green-eyed gaze on me as if
to say "Whadaya gonna do about it, Slick?
The child loves me and you love the child."

How to loathe something your child loves? How to rid the planet of the thing? How to do the perfect crime? And not get caught?

Truth told I really ought to have her "fixed"
in the old way, with an airtight alibi,
a bag of ready-mix and no eyewitnesses.
But one of these days she will lie there and be dead

Blessed assurance—there in that line—oh, what a foretaste of glory divine! This was my story, this was my song. The miserable cat's life wouldn't be long.

And choking back loud hallelujahs, I'll pretend
a brief bereavement for my Michael's sake,
letting him think, as he has often said
"Deep down inside you really love her don't you Dad?"
I'll even hold some cheerful obsequies
careful to observe God's never failing care
for even these, the least of His creatures,
making some mention of a cat-heaven where
cat-ashes to ashes, cat-dust to dust
and the Lord gives, and the Lord has taken away.

Yes, yes, I'd let Nature take its course! Patience and tolerance would win the day. I could be an example of forbearance to my children—a good father, a good man, good for something, after all!

Thus claiming my innocence to the end,
I'd turn Mike homeward from that wicked little grave
And if he asks, we'll get another one because
all boys need practice in the arts of love
and all their aging fathers in the arts of rage.

The poem was written in a day—a gray spring day gone blue, the buds on the magnolia busting loose, the boys out shooting hoops in the driveway, their sister sleeping in, whilst I was indoors disabusing myself of long years of contained contempt. It became the title poem for my second collection. Its words in my mouth were a kind deliverance from the yellow bile and the black bile and the disabling rage. I could live with the cat, or live without it. I could take or leave the thing and either way I didn't have to like it. And though I was left with the old dilemma—how not to love something your child does—all I needed to preserve was a home in which Michael could love the cat and love me, a thing he'd been managing well enough all along.

The children of divorce learn such divisions. I remember Michael in the first months of his parents' disaffections. We'd be out for groceries or riding down Main Street and he'd always want me to buy his mother flowers, or bring her home a gift, some surprise. He wanted me to woo her, to win her love back, to draw the distance in his little heart the nearer, to return his "selves" to himself by restoring the accord between his creators. Or he would say something really nice about his mother, about how she was the best at this or the best at that, and then he'd wait and watch and listen for my agreement—some hook on which to hang the little hope that we would not destroy the world he occupied. No doubt he did the same things with his mother. And as much as we loved him and his brothers and sister, as much as we would have done anything we could to spare them any hurt, in the end, we could not find a way to love each other anymore.

In the wars of divorce, it is children who pay the piper. Among the whole lies and half-truths my generation tells itself are the ones that say the kids are better off, or the kids will be fine, or that time heals all wounds. The kids are damaged. Some wounds won't heal. They may survive and thrive and learn to love themselves, but the harm that is done them is very, very real. Most divorces are not done to save lives or end abuses, or remedy interminable pain. There are those terrible few tinged by violence and madness, or persistent abuse or neglect, but the garden variety, amicably upmarket, suburban no-fault procedure common to my generation and our times, has less to do with life and death than with love and faith and fear and faithlessness. Most divorces are difficult choices in a world that applauds the exercise of choice, even the bad ones. And to have good reasons for divorce—as I did, as my former spouse would, no doubt, say she did, as we always do—does not make divorcing good. At its best it is the lesser of evils, a way to cut our losses, a way to say we couldn't keep the vows we made but we are still "okay." Whatever else it is, it is a shame that love contracted publicly with drinking and dancing and dressed to the nines is quit so quietly—a paper shuffle in the attorney's office, the grim facts filed with the county clerk, a hush long fallen over the crowd. It is the children who pay, for the two sets of parents and households, holidays and disciplines. However equal and amicable they might be, they are always separate, covertly at odds, subtly competing, quietly instructing in the separate and subversive dialects of love.

And though my former spouse got what she wanted and I got what I wanted, our children got, for the most part, divided between the love of their mother and the love of their father and the promises we made, in front of God and all those people, but did not keep. The parents got what they deserved. The children deserved some better than they got. And though I've heard and read every cheery argument to the contrary, I'd have to say it was like they were hobbled by it, the divorce, a kind of ball and chain they limped along with, then learned to walk with, then learned to run with, then ignored.

Though they learn to live with the damage, the damage done is permanent. It is not that their parents don't love them, it's that their parents do not love each other. Thus the children become beings divided against themselves. One parent's patience, the other's smile; Dad's sense of humor, Mom's sense of style—these incarnations become liabilities in the children of parents who no longer love each other. "You're just like your father" goes from appreciation to disparagement. What good to have your mother's eyes when your father does not love them?

ALL THAT WAS YEARS AGO now, the sadness and anger, the love and rage. The boy has grown into a man; his brothers and his sister likewise have grown lovely and capable, out beyond the orbit of their parents' choices. The cat is uglier, untidier, unrepentant as ever. The kids can vote and go to bars and fall in love and get their own credit. They live within the gravity of their own choices now. The cat roars and whines and will not be comforted. My gratitudes so far outnumber any grievances that most days and nights all I say is thanks to whatever God is listening for the safety of my sons and daughter. The cat is curled most days into a kind of fetal slumber between the legs of a table in the living room. It sleeps now more than anything. The boy who loves it most comes and goes. The cat remains.

Last year Mike was petting the cat and noticed some lumps in her hindquarters. "Cancer," I said, perhaps too gleefully, and said to take her to Dr. Clarke, the vet. I reckoned he'd recommend euthanasia. But Mike returned, bearing the cat like a newborn in his arms, saying it was only burrs and fur balls and such. They'd shaved the cat from the midsection back so that it came out looking like the Lion King, its little bald rump a spectacle. It cost $160 to find out the cat was badly groomed and was not dying.

Last spring it was nearly finished. I'd been emailing Mike for weeks at school, telling him about the cat's bad leg, how the arthritis seemed to be especially vexing to her, how her cataracts were becoming more cloudy, her deafness more pronounced, her miseries more noisome, her toilet habits more free-ranging. I told Mike something merciful would have to be considered. He said nothing. It hurt me to think of how it would hurt him. Still, he understood the difficult decisions that were facing him.

I called Dr. Clarke. There followed a highly professional discussion on the nature of pain and palliative care and incapacity. The poor cat, I told him, could hardly move and was puking and oozing from every orifice and that Mike was coming home for the Easter break and that "the right thing would have to be done." Dr. Clarke, ever the empathist, ever the compassionate professional, set an appointment for Saturday at one P.M.

And everything was going more or less according to plan. The cat looked especially haggard. Mike was sad and resolute. It was the doctor's last appointment for the day. It was a good day for the cat to die. I'd ordered in a wee box for the occasion and even had a stone cut with the cat's name and dates—*1978–1999*—a tasteful little twenty-by-ten-by-four-inch memorial in a dense eastern granite, to mark the space already dug in the back garden where all of Mike's more normally mortal pets were buried. The cold granite waited in the garage, the box beside it, everything in readiness. I'd left an eleven o'clock funeral service early to go with Mike. I wanted to "be there" for him, the way that dads are supposed to do. Even the cat seemed resigned to her fate.

And Dr. Clarke, a boon to man and beast alike, was saying all the right things about how "nothing lives forever" and how Mike had been such a "loyal friend" and how he'd have to do the "right thing," however painful, here at the end. And they were both nodding their heads in sad consensus, and the cat's head was nodding too, and I was nodding mine as well, and Mike's brave face was reddening and his eyes were welling up, and maybe it was the sight of this big, abundantly handsome young man holding his cat, holding back the big sob, and one tear working its way down his cheekbone, that was more than even Dr. Clarke and his attendant nurse could handle. I don't know, but whatever it was I heard Dr. Clarke stammer something about "perhaps a shot of cortisone," how maybe that would offer some "relief," how maybe it would give her some "quality of life," and I was thinking that it had better be one massive overdose of cortisone, because inside my head I'm screaming *NO, NO—IT'S NOT QUALITY OF LIFE WE CAME FOR*, because I'm counting on the cat to be dead tonight. I'd all but ordered up the cake and coffee. But Mike, with this little hand of hope extended, was nodding, yes, yes, that would at least give him time to finish the semester at school, you know, and spend more quality time with the cat, and I was still thinking the vet was just kidding about all of this when the nurse returned with Kleenex for Mike and a hypodermic that was given to the cat and the cat didn't die, not then, not since, and, in fact, she has begun to get a little bounce back in her limp and she shits in the kitty litter now and the old toms are appearing at the back door again and she sleeps all day and roars all night and grins at me as if she knew all along that the pardon and reprieve were set.

But here's the thing. The thing she doesn't know. The stone is cut. It is out there in the garage with her name and dates on it, and *1999* is what it says.

And I'm not one to make a liar out of stones.

Which is why if she won't die by natural causes or some household calamity, then, by all that's holy, the last thing I'll do in this millennium is drop that blunt lump of gray granite, all fifty or sixty pounds of it, on that godawful gray cat before the New Year turns. Whether the ball drops in Times Square, planes fall from the sky or lights go out around the globe; whether banks fail, phones fall silent; whether the world ends with a bang or a whimper; whether the earth or sea give up their dead; whatever happens or doesn't happen, call it mercy or murder, call me crazy or Katvorkian, by the first dawn of the New Age the old cat will be out of my life and times forever. I promise. By the time you read this the cat will be dead.

The Big Enchilada

The news, lately reported, that the life span of humans might be doubled in the next century, is cause for sober and deliberate contemplation. Like so much that is baffling and wondrous, the word comes from a conference in southern California. Dr. Gregory Stock of the School of Medicine at UCLA, encouraged by successes with roundworms and fruit flies, bats and canaries and different-sized mice, impaneled his colleagues in the allied sciences to discuss what one of the attendees calls "the big enchilada"—the prospect of humans reconfigured to live 150 or 200 years. Genetic tampering and evolutionary microengineering seem to be the most promising methods.

What seems on the face of it rude good news is coincidental with or correlated to the news that things are dismal in the "funeral futures" market. Once the darlings of Wall Street, the death-care conglomerate has been bankrupted, downsized, and downgraded by what is at once the good news and the bad news of the industry—everyone is going to die once. But only once. The stocks have fallen precipitously. Lawsuits have been filed by disgruntled investors. Before his hasty "retirement," the former CEO, L. William Heiligbrodt, said, "Declining death rates pose a challenge for the industry." We live in oxymoronic times. People are living longer but suffering diminishing returns on their mortuary investments. Time, it turns out, is not money. More is less.

Surely, the big enchilada can be blamed.

The big enchilada, such as it is, is near enough within our grasp that Dr. Stock and Company pose what seems a sensible question, to wit: "Given adequate funding, given lucky breaks, how far could we go?"

Let me hazard that "too far" is one of the possible answers. We are a species, and especially a country, for whom, like drunks with drink or politicos with other peoples' money, enough is never going to be enough. It was true of the arms race, deficit spending and TV violence, the impeachment hearings and high-tech stocks—our appetites are insatiable, our habits tend toward gluttony and incontinence. That less-is-more, minimalist, eco-friendly, paradigm-shifting, salt-free Zen blather about stopping to smell the roses and quality time might be good for the shrink's office or the downsized employees of the structured buyout, but if the age of merger and acquisition has taught us anything, it is that less is unacceptable, bigger is better, more than anything we want more.

Here at the funeral home I operate in middle America, our favorite parlor game is Demographics and Expectancies. We play between the local obsequies. It bears a semblance to Trivial Pursuit. In the last century, the life expectancy of my fellow citizens rose from forty-seven to seventy-six years. Such wonders can be credited to antibiotics, indoor plumbing, spandex and the soybean.

With the extra three decades in most of our lives, we neither cured the common cold nor secured peace in the Balkans, but we did invent the Wonderbra and no-load mutual funds. With all this extra time to kill, we went to war more, watched more TV and spent more time at the therapist's or shopping mall than any of the short-lived generations before us. We also golfed more and gambled more and built more and safer and more fuel-efficient Buicks and Boeings that got us farther and faster to more and more distant places that seemed, once we got there, more crowded somehow. And, though we liberated more of the planet, educated more of our citizens, vaccinated more of our children and empowered many of the formerly disenfranchised; though we increased the minimum wage, exported Coca-Cola and Disney World, put men on the moon and women in the paid workforce, the returns on the extra life expectancy are mixed. We are taller, stronger, healthier and live longer than our parents or their parents, for no apparent reason. And like our parents and their parents, we will surely die. The numbers on this last fact are convincing.

If our great-grandchildren will have to wait till 90 for the hard-won sense that came to us at 45, if they must endure double the incremental damages of serial monogamy, the twenty-four-hour news cycle, easy-listening music, Tae Bo and infomercials, talking heads and TV preachers, gender-norming and sexual politics, no amount of Ritalin or Prozac or Viagra will make them "well," however fit they seem to be at 150.

Maybe instead of doubling our already world-record life spans, we might labor for existential parity in the Third World. Maybe we could add a decade to Nepal, where the life expectancy is 55, or Guatemala, where it is 62, or Estonia, where it is 65. Perhaps we should spend some of our "adequate funding" and "lucky breaks" and see just how far we can go in, say, leveling the life-span playing field between white and black Americans, rich and poor Americans, male and female Americans, Americans with and without health coverage.

To the medicos peddling the enchilada and the pre-need sales counselor who wants to sell us our funerals in advance, maybe "Thanks but no thanks" is the thing we should say—as if we had learned to spread the wealth or leave such decisions to our children, or, failing that, to leave well enough alone.

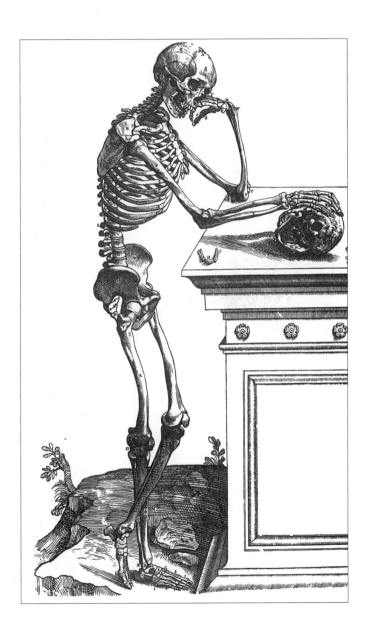

The Oak Grove
Imbroglio

L ately, the local citizenry is vexed by questions of "usage" in the village graveyard. It seems nothing is self-evident anymore.

Thespians with time on their hands can be a peril. Years ago there'd have been factories and wars and children underfoot to fatigue them, but now they all have 401Ks and flex time, day care and Planned Parenthood and the Pax Americana. Add to this expanding idleness the appetites of history buffs and the booster-ism of chamber-of-commerce types and we get a sometimes toxic cocktail of "good ideas." There is a hybrid class of do-gooder on the loose for whom even the dead are not past improvement, godhelp-us. Just such a consortium came up with the brainstorm, over the winter, for what they call a Cemetery Walk to disturb the peace of the third weekend in August on what they hope will be an annual basis.

They used to do this play in Central Park, under a big tent rented for the weekend. They called it *Milford Memories*. It was mostly about the good old days and the good old-timers who used to live here a good old century ago before sidewalks and indoor plumbing and Internet access made life complex. A band was hired, costumes made, lines learned at rehearsals. Posters were put up all around town. Tickets were sold in the local emporia. Mention was made from several pulpits.

The first year, of course, everyone came to see what their neighbors had wrought. The next year no one came back, not even for the free matinee on Sunday afternoon. Apparently the fascination with Victoriana has its limits and the local curiosities had been sated. The old days, it turns out, are a finite field of study. Even when it is costumed, dramatized and set to music, it is hard to compete with twentieth-century spectacles. The writers blamed the actors, the actors blamed the writers. Both groups looked with suspicion at the band.

It is a long-established truth of the theater that if the script cannot be improved upon and the actors are working at the top of their craft and still no one comes, then it must be the venue, the stage. If the *what* and *who* cannot be fixed, maybe the *where* is worth another look. This is when someone proposed a "Cemetery Walk." The troop turned its collective head as a water spaniel will when a strange noise is heard.

"We could do it in Oak Grove!" the visionary said. "Who needs props when you've got headstones and monuments, the names and dates and everything right there!"

Some naysayer said it would be hard to get folks to show up at a graveyard.

"Not if you take them by buckboard wagons!" said one of the crew. A certain contagion attends such brainstorms. "We could sell lemonade!" said another.

The hitherto crestfallen cast members began to nod and smile at one another. Same costumes, same script, same camaraderie, but a new and improved "stage." The director, who manages a local real estate franchise, said, "Location, location, location!"

An organizing committee was formed. One of the thespians was active with the Historical Society, which unanimously agreed to act as co-sponsor of the event. Another knew someone on the township board, which promptly granted its permission to use the cemetery without public hearing, for surely no one would take issue with such a worthy enterprise. A route was established to take advantage of the best old houses with their gingerbread and formal gardens. Banners and buntings appeared. The wholesale syndication of good intentions, good neighbors and good times resembled nothing so much as one of those Brueghel prints in which happy villagers turn their efforts to a common purpose, like *Hay Making* or *The Peasant Dance* or *Children's Games*, and live happily ever after.

When the day in August itself arrived, tickets were sold for seats in horse-drawn wagons hired from the local 4-H crowd that made their leisurely way through the old section of town, with docents from the Historical Society riding shotgun, pointing out en route some points of historical significance, architectural importance and local lore until they came to Oak Grove Cemetery, where actors in period costumes and paste-on beards jumped out from behind the headstones of our historical dead and told their stories. Civil war casualties, flu victims and Main Street merchants long since dead were "brought to life," so to speak, to a more or less captive audience of variously bewildered and wide-eyed wagoneers who, conditioned by the culture they lived in, felt, nonetheless, "entertained" or "edified" or, at the very least, part of a "meaningful shared experience."

The writers, directors and actors all agreed that the production was, well, "moving." That this may have had something to do with the horse-drawn wagons was a truth that remained, all the same, unspoken. The costly band had been replaced by taped music and a boom box. The tent rental and chair rental had been made redundant. To the extent that the ticket sales covered the cost of the livery charges, a little stipend to the cemetery maintenance fund and the wine-and-cheese cast party that inevitably followed, the project was fashioned a monumental if break-even success!

So it was with great distress that they received the news, in the form of a letter to the *Milford Times* the following week, that some of the people who had family buried in Oak Grove took issue with the use of their ancestors' final resting place as a "stage" of sorts. Had the organizers of this production no sense of decorum or respect for the dead?

But what better way to commemorate the dead, it was argued, than to educate the living about their lives? The place is full of history and "characters" and stories and art!

No, the other side argued, it is full of fathers and mothers and daughters and sons who have no obligation to educate or entertain or instruct the living. Museums and libraries, art galleries and public parks, serve these purposes. The bodies of the dead make Oak Grove a sacred space. The lessons of the grave are taught in stony quiet to those who go there for their hushed reasons, less for information than for contemplation, less for soliloquy than for interior monologue.

The thespians argued the merits of the play, its dignity and respect and artistic splendors, its value as a vehicle for history and local interests.

LOCATION, LOCATION, LOCATION, came the counter-charge. The right thing done in the wrong place is, in the end, a mistake. There are plenty of options available to the living. The high school, the Methodist church, the Masonic temple, all have stages. Central Park has an amphitheater and plentiful parking. The dead, long buried, are grounded, optionless, rooted to their graves in ways that could not be relieved or remedied. The issue of *choice* has reared its contentious head with shades of *Hamlet* and the late-century debates over zoning and privacy and barrier-free access.

Then there's the matter, ever a concern in the Middle West, of the slippery slope. If a Cemetery Walk for the Historical Society, why not a Cemetery Bird Watching for the Audubon Society? What possible harm is there in bird watching? If a Cemetery Walk for Milford Memories, why not a 5-K run through the cemetery to raise funds for disabled veterans? Is that not a noble purpose? What possible harm in a 5-K run? If a Cemetery Walk for the sake of history, why not a memorial band concert—what possible harm? And if a band concert, why not a folk concert, and if a folk concert, why not a rock concert, and if rock, why not reggae or rap or a bit of opera—who gets to choose, who gets to say which kind of concert is and isn't appropriate? Or why not a bake sale or wine tasting or memorial raft race—for Oak Grove is bordered by the mighty Huron too? Why not art shows or poetry readings or nature studies or ecology lectures? Why oughtn't the Rotary Club, which has several past members buried there, and an interest in the heritage of this place, have an annual picnic there to raise awareness about this town and the Rotary's involvement with it? Or why not the PTA, or the chamber of commerce, or the Thursday night bowling league? There's never a shortage of interest and a worthy cause. These are all good things, undertaken by good people for all the best reasons. And Oak Grove might well seem a good place for them. What possible harm?

The harm, of course, is that once the gate is opened it is hard to close, and lost forever is the sacred and dedicated space that is only a cemetery and needs be nothing more.

The Oak Grove imbroglio won't be settled soon. There's never a shortage of polemic or opinion here. Low inflation and a bull market have left us all with time on our hands to ponder the formerly imponderable questions. Should a graveyard be a graveyard only? Whose cemetery is it anyway? Are the dead left in the livings' care or in their indenture?

The village council has put the matter on the agenda for its October meeting. There will be a series of public hearings. Fund-raisers are scheduled on both sides of the questions. Placards are being painted in folks' garages. The newspaper is planning a special series of reports.

Maybe if I took a funeral down through town—hearse and limousines, corpse and pallbearers, family and friends, cast and crew, all of us playing our long-practiced parts—but took a detour into Central Park and laid the dead guy out in the gazebo there and engaged one of the local clergy to hold forth on the mysteries of death and the promise of salvation, or buried the next few clients in the tennis courts, or burned a few locals in the barbecue and scattered their ashes in the horseshoe pits, or consigned the bodies to the deep of the wee pond there, or set them adrift on a blazing barge, Viking-style, in the middle of the mighty Huron River, which runs along the south edge of the village green; maybe folks would start to understand. If Oak Grove can be turned into a theater, can't Central Park be memorial gardens? Even the most noble of human endeavors can miss the mark by half a mile sometimes. Is there a chance the thespians will get the picture?

Still, maybe they'd turn up with their video-cams and patio chairs—ever ready for the movie version of a good idea—giving out with "Places everyone! Lights. Camera. Quiet on the set. Roll 'em!"

Nora

Even now, here thirty years since, when I turn to the southwest in Ennis from Shannon, and head out the peninsula that ends at Loop Head, and somewhere on that road get my first wind of turfsmoke, I remember the first time and the sense that I had then of coming home.

"The name's good," the man in the customs hall had said, letting my bag pass without a look. I had a hundred dollars in my pocket, the stub of a one-way ticket from Detroit to Shannon and the whereabouts of my cousins, much removed, committed to memory: *Moveen West, Kilkee, County Clare*. It was February 1970. I was twenty-one.

MY KNOWLEDGE OF PEOPLE and a home in West Clare "on the banks of the River Shannon" began over Sunday dinners at my grandparents'. To the grace he would recite before turkey and gravy, my grandfather would add, "And don't forget your cousins Tommy and Nora Lynch on the banks of the River Shannon, don't forget." Then we would sit and pass the dishes, the people and place names familiar and mysterious, like prayers we learn to say before we learn the meaning of them.

He himself had never met them—Tommy and Nora, his first cousins, son and daughter of his father's brother. His father, my great-grandfather, another Tom Lynch, had left West Clare in the 1890s and come to Jackson, Michigan, for steady work in the prison there and the Studebaker factory. He never returned to Ireland. Nor had my grandfather or father. I was the first back. My mother's people, O'Haras from Sligo and Graces from Kilkenny, had lost all interest in or knowledge of their townlands. And my father's people, most of a century and four thousand miles removed, hung by this little ritual thread of remembrance—*Bless us, O Lord . . . Tommy and Nora . . . banks of the Shannon . . . don't forget.*

SOME THINGS CHANGE and some things don't. The thatch on that cottage in 1970 gave way to slate and the great open hearth has been enclosed and storage heaters and back boiler installed. The water that was brought by buckets from down the land and boiled in the coals runs hot and cold now in the sink and shower. There are more appliances and less cooking somehow. There's a phone and a toilet and a TV—the great civilizers of the twentieth century. But the flagstones are the same, the thick walls, the deep windows, the wind off the ocean, the dark of night, the cattle in the cow cabins, the turf in the shed, the names of the families up and down the road.

Tommy died the year after I met him and Nora lived on, a sound woman on her own there until she died, almost ninety, in 1992. She changed my life. I think I changed hers. I was her Yank, the one who came back albeit generations late, and kept coming back year after year, with news of America and her American family. And after her brother died she made her first trip to Dublin to get her visa to go herself and see the place where her sisters and cousins had gone. She made five trips in all to the States, the last the summer before she died. She left the house, her home, to me. It was the home my great-grandfather left a century ago and never saw again. And sometimes sitting in the west window there, I see what that Tom Lynch must have seen, looking out at Newtown and the sea coming up in Goleen and the mouth of the Shannon agape in the southwest—a topography that he looked past for his future, and the one I look on with a sense of the past. He left Clare with a tin footlocker with TOM LYNCH—WANTED on it. He left with most of his life in front of him but few choices. I return, twice a year, most years now, with most of my life lived but with many more options. I get *The Irish Times* on-line and the *Clare Champion* in the mail. I bring tea back in my suitcase and get books mailed from Kenny's in Galway. I have email and phone calls from my neighbors in West Clare. Here or there I'm never far from home.

And sometimes, sitting there, warming my hands to the fire, I think of Nora sitting, warming hers, and remember how her faith was informed by doubt and wonder. "I wonder if there's anything at all," she'd say. "I wonder if He hears us when we pray." Nora had a fierce heart, long years and the sense that life repeats itself. "'Twas Tom that went," she'd say, "and Tom that would come back."

Reno

S o I'm sitting in the casino of
the Reno Hilton on the twenty-first of June, 1999. It is the
summer solstice, the end of the age. And I've lengthened the light
of the longest day by boarding a jet and flying westward from
Michigan, where this morning I woke up at four o'clock. I've seen
the sunup in Milford in Eastern Daylight Time and the sundown
from my room on the twenty-fourth floor, dipping below the
mountains into the Pacific—nearly twenty hours of blessed light.

Maybe it was the catnap in coach class, or maybe it's the accu-
mulated lag from too many jets, or maybe the certain knowledge
that the days will indeed be getting shorter—solstice and equinox,
time and light—or maybe it's the coffee. I don't know.

Whatever the reasons, here I am nearing midnight in Reno
mindlessly playing the dollar slots in a room full of conventioneers
and crazies and insomniacs: strangely expressionless people, neither happy nor sad but more or less numb. And we're, all of us,
basking in the manufactured lights of PAYDAY and JACKPOT and
MEGABUCKS blinking wildly from the banks of machines, the

space beaming with chandeliers, neon icons and images everywhere. And there is some nonspecific late-century pop music coming out of the ceiling and the occasional voice-over informing us of the "All-you-can-eat crab-and-shrimp buffet served nightly for only 10.99," and an underdin of oddly comforting bells and whistles and electrical signals all mixing together in a kind of babel. I'm pressing the buttons, the way I'm supposed to, watching the sevens and cherries and double and triple bars twirling round and round, giving and taking away the money. And everything is blinking and blurring and buzzing with bright assurances, like there's no tomorrow, and I should let it ride, and I'm wondering if everyone here is wondering the way I'm wondering now—*what exactly are we doing here?*

THE DAYS ARE GETTING SHORTER. It is later than we think.

I'M HERE AT THE INVITE of the California Funeral Directors Association, which has convened its annual meeting here. There's something for everyone in the family. While Dad is doing committee work and inspecting caskets at the exhibit hall, the kids can play downstairs in the nickel arcade and Mom can play blackjack for big bucks or browse in the mall. There are side trips to Tahoe and Virginia City, a golf outing and other organized events. I'm here to deliver the keynote speech in the morning—to tell them what it is exactly that we're doing here.

Last week I was in Rotterdam for the thirtieth annual Poetry International—poets, translators, editors, publishers, from every corner of the spoken word, invited to the Low Countries for a weeklong festival.

And the week before that it was Kentucky for the undertakers, and the week before that, Scotland and Ireland on the poetry biz, and the month before that, a kind of midwestern, Buddy Holly tour of mortuary conventions—five states in six days—and the week before that one, some poetry jobs at Eau Claire and Winona and Williamsburg, Virginia. All of it's a litany now of literary and mortuary confabs that stretch back through the winter and fall of last year—Belfast and Barcelona; Galway and Boston; Glasgow, Manhattan and Amsterdam; Ocean City; Rapid City; Seattle; Atlantic City; Edinburgh; San Francisco; Denver and Atlanta; London and Dundee and Cornwall and Dublin and Portland and Chicago and Philly and D.C.; and Bozeman, Montana; Indianapolis; Minneapolis; Wichita, Kansas; godhelpus—blather and racket until I'm all but struck dumb with it and these blinking lights that are all beginning to blend together now into a kind of blindness. The more of the planet I see, the less I see it.

Maybe it is time to get some sleep.

Among my writerly friends, the hushed talk eventually comes round to the fact that I'm a funeral director. How is it, they want to know, that someone who writes sonnets also embalms, sells caskets, drives a hearse and greets the mourners at the door? It strikes them a strange commingling: the mortuary and literary arts. Why, they wonder, don't I take up a day job teaching grad students something meaningful about dactyls and pentameters at the university?

Among my fellow funeral directors, I am likewise suspect. There are dark rumors about bookish and artistic "types"—a wariness that owes, I suppose, to Mitford and Waugh—a mistrust of wordsmiths and journalists. Why, they wonder, don't I take up golf or the stock market, boating or Web browsing?

Of course, my publishers have made some hay off this, to their advantage and to mine. An "undertaker/poet," like a cop who sings opera or a wrestler turned governor, makes for good copy and easy interviews. Oddity and celebrity are near enough cousins. Ink and airtime—coin of the realm in the info-tainment industry—are easier when you have a quirky angle.

Much the same, the mortuary associations have put me on the "circuit" of state and national conventions, where I'm fresh fodder for the programs and exhibit committees. After years of psycho-babblers and marketing gurus dispensing warm-fuzzies and motivationals, a reading and book signing by a "poet and author and one of our own" has a certain panache.

I charge accordingly, as any dancing bear would do.

BUT HERE'S THE QUIET LITTLE TRUTH of the matter. Requiems and prosodies, sonnets and obsequies, poems and funerals—they are all the same. The arrangement of flowers and homages, casseroles and sympathies; the arrangement of images and idioms, words on a page—it is all the same—an effort at meaning and metaphor, an exercise in symbol and ritualized speech, the heightened acoustics of language raised against what is reckoned unspeakable—faith and heartbreak, desire and pain, love and grief, the joyous and sorrowful mysteries by which we keep track of our lives and times.

Sometimes I see in the stillness of the dead the blank space between stanzas, the held breath of inspiration, the silence that rhymes with almost anything. The math of each enterprise is imprecise—wholesale, retail, rhyme and meter, the counting of syllables, the tally of charges: all numbers games that end in bottom lines. Still, the words we cut in stone or shape in poems are worth more, somehow, than the usual palaver.

A good funeral, like a good poem, is driven by voices, images, intellections and the permanent. It moves us up and back the cognitive and imaginative and emotive register. The transport seems effortless, inspired, natural as breathing or the loss of it. In the space between what is said and unsaid, in the pause between utterances, whole histories are told; whole galaxies are glimpsed in the margins, if only momentarily. At wakes and in verse, both absence and presence inform the work. What is said and what is unsaid are both instructive. The elegist and eulogist must both attend to the adverbs, be sparing with the adjectives, be mindful of the changing tense of predicates and have a sense of when enough is enough. The fashions in verse-making and leave-taking are always changing while the fundamental witness remains the same. Good poems and good funerals are stories well told.

It is likewise so that we poets and funeral directors have a fondness for black, the keening of pipers, irregular hours, free drink and horizontal bodies. Our children uniformly report that we often seem distracted. Our spouses endure our bouts of passion and distemper, egomania and inferiority. Whether we err on the side of excess or meanness, when we miss the point, we miss it badly.

We are all the same. And no two are alike. Dante's *Commedia*, Grant's Tomb, your child's first quatrain, your one and only mother's death, your father's.

• • •

WHENEVER FUNERAL DIRECTORS GET TOGETHER they talk about the fact that no one likes funerals. Whenever poets get together they talk about the fact that no one likes poetry. Co-misery plays a big part in their get-togethers. There are worries over audience interest and the marketplace.

For poetry readings the general rule is that if the poet is outnumbered, it is a success. If outnumbered by a dozen or more, it is a huge success. A crowd like the crowds they turn up in Rotterdam—hundreds to listen to the likes of me or Lorna Goodison from Jamaica or Chen Li from Taiwan or Haji Gora Haji from Zanzibar—such multitudes will be mentioned in our obituaries. "He once filled the Rotterdam City Theatre," it will read, a tasteful dose of hyperbole, "with people hungry for his poems." Lost to literary history will be the three Dubliners who turned out to Bewley's in Grafton Street one Wednesday in October some years ago—my driver, "the events organizer" and one fetching young woman we took to be a discerning reader, but it turned out she was actually lost.

The same rule holds for funerals. Wherever two or three are gathered is enough to outnumber the dead guy. If one of them will stand up and hold forth, you've got all the ingredients you will ever need: someone who agrees to quit breathing, someone who cares, and someone who's trying to make some sense of all of this. Half a dozen and they can carry the dead one to the final resting place. More than a hundred makes it an "exceptional tribute," especially on a weekday when the weather is bad.

And though poetry and funerals have been around for a while, there's the sense that their ancient forms may not be relevant to the postmodern, postindustrial, 24-7 televised news cycle of a deconstructed, digital world where everything is wired and managed by mouse-click and mass-marketed or geared to a niche or a focus group or a poll and anyone who wants to be one of the players better play by the numbers and compete for space and offend no one and appeal to a crowd and hold their attention, keep them entertained enough to keep them from changing channels, or keep them anesthetized enough so that they'll think they're getting something for their money, like these folks here in Reno, there at the two-for-one bar, and here at the sure-bet slots, and there at the all-you-can-eat buffet.

Last week in Rotterdam, for example, Poetry International was opened with a "Defense of Poetry"—a kind of keynote speech—by the Mongolian poet and shaman Galsan Tschinag, a Tuvan tribal chief. His native language having no script, he writes in German, which he learned in Leipzig. He sings in Tuvinian. His defense of poetry ran about an hour. Translations were available in booklets in the lobby afterward. Several dozen copies were given away. Everyone applauded and nodded and smiled.

Perhaps if they shot a poet, or hanged one, or banished one to some hinterland like they used to in the old days when language was dangerous and words were magic and poets weren't tenured but they weren't ignored, the attention and attendance would be better. The poems would reach a broader audience. Dead poets always fare better than live ones. Better yet if one was burned at the stake. At least the media would turn up for the show: the roving reporters, the poetry-cam, the talking heads to tell us what we heard and saw.

AND ONE OF THE WORKSHOPS here in Reno will certainly sound like a "Defense of Funerals." Some Ph.D. or M.D. or M.S.W. will tell the F.D.'s all about the "Value of the Funeral."

Maybe if funerals hadn't been so co-opted by the grief therapists and memorial counselors, the pie-in-the-skyers and casket peddlers; maybe if it was about more than our "feelings" or our "salvation" or our disposal. Maybe if funerals were a whole-being enterprise: something for our flesh and fears and faith and for the dead. If we burned them in public or buried them ourselves or bore them through town giving thanks and praise, making peace with the powers of God and Nature in carefully worded lamentations, incantations, benedictions, we would have to defend neither poetry nor funerals. We would simply do them whenever the spirits, the living or the dead ones, moved us to.

When, I wonder, do things become self-evident.

Poetry tunes our senses to the language. Without it how could we bear the Information Age and all its words, its lists of options, its multiple choices, its idiot menus from which we must make our selections? And funerals tune our senses to our mortal nature; like proper punctuation, whether we end with exclamation, questions or full stop, they lend meaning to our lives, our human being. Both press our attention to the existentials, the adverbials, the sensual and overwhelming questions, the mysteries and certainties of life and death.

Maybe it is because we have removed the poems and the corpses from our daily rounds. We are glad to have poets in the way we are glad to have good infrastructure. Smooth roads, clean drinking water, a sestina now and then—we are willing to pay the millage so that we can ignore them. We tuck them into universities with living wages and dental coverage and the captive audience of our sons and daughters. We are glad they are writing poems and gladder still that we needn't read them. We give them grants and sabbaticals, a little airtime on the radio, a little shelf space in the corner of the megastore, and otherwise expect them to be still and disappear into the larger lifescapes of politics, history, events and entertainments, self-help and diet fads.

Much as we want the dead and dying to be still and disappear. Though we are drawn to the movies and the evening news with their murders and virtual blood and gore, and though the mort-cam is always at the ready to hover overhead the latest tragedy or terrorism; though prepackaged, media-approved, commercially viable opportunities abound for "national" mourning, surrogate sadnesses and remote-control grief, our locally dying and our local dead, our real-life family and friends, are, for the most part, disappeared—their bodies quickly hidden or disposed of in the name of efficiency and dignity, privacy and convenience. The actual, palpable, slowly decomposing and tangible facts of the matter are declared irrelevant, like good infrastructure, like poetry.

I REMEMBER THE FIRST POEM I ever heard, the first dead human body I ever saw. Neither scarred my psyche but each changed my life. Each gave it meaning by holding forth a mystery.

Angel of God, my guardian dear,
to whom God's love commits me here,
ever this day be at my side
to light to guard to rule and guide.

My mother taught me to say this poem morning, noon and night. I hadn't a clue what it meant exactly, but the jaunty progress toward its echoes pleased my ear. The sense that its syllables, the saying of them, held powerful medicine and protections proceeded from that pleasure, then as now.

The first dead person I remember seeing was an old man on the table of the embalming room at my father's office. I was ten, I think, or thereabouts. My father had taken me to work with him on a Saturday. The embalming room was at the back of the old funeral home. We entered by the back door off the alley. I wasn't told I was about to see a dead body or that it should do me any damage, or that there were any preparations I should make emotionally. I was only going to work with my father. I knew his work involved the dead as sons of doctors know their parents deal with sickness or the children of clergy have heard of sin, as every child is aware of sex—the idea of the thing but not the thing itself. I remember that the room smelled like the doctor's office and the figure on the table was covered by a sheet except for his head, his face. The sheet was white, the table was white, the face was white and it was quiet. There was a stillness about that body unlike anything I'd witnessed in nature before. His head was bald, his eyes and mouth were closed, his nose was large, as were his earlobes. I asked my father what his name was, what his age was, what he died of and if he had children. And though I can't remember the particulars, I remember that my father gave me answers. He also said that I should say a prayer. I wasn't frightened but I was changed.

And sometimes I wonder what my life would have been if not for dead bodies and dead poets.

"When you are old and gray and full of sleep/and nodding by the fire take down this book . . ." William Butler Yeats wrote in his memorable pentameters to Maud Gonne, whom he loved and who wouldn't have him a century ago. He had, in his youth, the certain sense that these lines and others like them would survive their youth, their age, their century. They have. The great Irish master bridged the nineteenth and twentieth centuries with poetry of such power and appeal that instructions written but months before his death ring true and timely still:

> *Irish poets, learn your trade,*
> *Sing whatever is well made,*
> *Scorn the sort now growing up*
> *All out of shape from toe to top . . .*

It is the meter and rhyme scheme of Yeats's late poem that W. H. Auden, not quite thirty-two when Yeats died on January 28, 1939, echoed in his famous elegy "In Memory of W. B. Yeats":

> *Earth, receive an honored guest;*
> *William Yeats is laid to rest:*
> *Let the Irish vessel lie*
> *Emptied of its poetry.*
>
> *Time that is intolerant*
> *Of the brave and innocent,*
> *And indifferent in a week*
> *To a beautiful physique,*
>
> *Worships language and forgives*
> *Everyone by whom it lives;*
> *Pardons cowardice, conceit,*
> *Lays its honours at their feet.*

I was among the fortunate hundreds who heard Seamus Heaney—one by whom the language lives—in Galway's Town Hall Theatre a few Aprils ago during the Cuirt Festival of Literature. The Nobel laureate, noting this borrowing of Yeats's meter and rhyme, paraphrased Auden to the effect that "poetry is what we do to break bread with the dead." And extending Auden's metaphor, Heaney added, "If so, then surely rhyme and meter are the table manners." He is, of course, correct.

Poetry is a kind of communion, the chore of ordinary talk made sacramental by the attention to what is memorable, transcendent, permanent, in the language. It is the common tongue by which the species remains connected to the past and bears its witness to the future. Each age offers variations on the themes of love and grief, reason and desire, prayer and homage, epic and elegy and honor. Some things are constantly changing. Some things never do. Poets and their poetry keep track of each.

But before it was a written and read thing, poetry was a spoken and said thing that happened in the ears and mouth before the eyes and intellect were engaged. It belonged to the body as much as the mind. It earned its place by pleasuring the senses. Before there were daily papers and news anchors and talking heads, there were bards who made their way from village to village bearing the news—*Who was king in the next county; who stole whose cow; who slept with whose wife; who slaughtered whose son.* And they were paid, well paid, to praise in verse a comely bride, a valiant warrior, a loyal dog; and paid to curse the blackguard, the enemy and the enemy's gods. And all of this was done out loud—for the sound and sense of it—the way we sing in the shower, practice our proposals and listen for our own voice before we fall asleep at night. Rhyme and meter were tools of the trade, a way of making words memorable and memorizable, a pace tied to the footfall of the poets' journeys.

We are drawn to the acoustic pleasures of poetry by nature and metabolism. Our hearts beat in iambs and trochees night and day. Our breath is caught between inspiration and expiration. Our pulse divided by our breathing equals the five-finger-tapping pentameters of Frost: "The land was ours before we were the land's." And Shakespeare: "From forth the fatal loins of these two foes." And Millay: "What lips my lips have kissed, and where, and why." Is it any wonder that we know these things by heart?

Our first petitions are learned by rhyme and meter: "Now I lay me down to sleep/and pray the Lord my soul to keep." Our first benedictions: "God is great, God is good/Let us thank Him for our food." Our first mysteries: "Twinkle, twinkle, little star/How I wonder what you are." Our first mastery: "A B C D E F G/H I J K lmno P." Our first formula: "Red sky at morning/Sailor take warning/Red sky at night/Sailor's delight." Our first poem, memorized: "Tyger! Tyger! burning bright/In the forests of the night,/What immortal hand or eye?/Could frame thy fearful symmetry?"

If this meter of William Blake's became Yeats's late instruction to Irish poets, and later Auden's elegy for Yeats, it serves as well for Seamus Heaney's lament for Joseph Brodsky, the Russian exile and fellow Nobel laureate who learned to write in English and died too young on January 28, 1996. Giving his poems in Galway that spring, Heaney took up his place at the table of poets who will outlive their centuries. With impeccable manners and in a well-tested form, he paid his respects to his dead friend, to old masters and to their ancient craft in "Audenesque—In Memory of Joseph Brodsky."

> Joseph, yes, you know the beat.
> Wystan Auden's metric feet
> Marched to it, unstressed and stressed,
> Laying William Yeats to rest.

Therefore, Joseph, on this day,
Yeats' anniversary,
(Double-crossed and death-marched date,
January twenty-eight),

Its measured ways I tread again
Quatrain by constrained quatrain,
Meting grief and reason out
As you said a poem ought.

Trochee, trochee, falling: thus
Grief and metre order us.
Repetition is the rule,
Spins on lines we learnt at school.

Heaney's poem, which gathers power and sorrow for another dozen quatrains, will be part, no doubt, of a future collection. It is good to be alive while this man is writing. It is good to hear his voice in two millennia.

But well-made poems outlive their makers and slip the restraints of ordinary time to become confluent with language at its source, all those tributaries of the human voice, in all its dialects, vernaculars and patois; wellsprings that rise to the species' thirst for metaphor.

Last month in a schoolhouse on the edge of the ocean in West Clare a student raised his hand to ask me, "Sir, what age did ye get your poetic license?" His classmates giggled, his kindly teacher grinned and blushed. But the boy himself was dead serious. He knew it was something that gave you privileges and special powers, like driving the tractor or fishing the cliffs, or serving the priest at Sunday Masses. I told him I was born with it. I told him he was too—born with it—and he should never lose it, his poetic license, his voice, his ear for this life's griefs and meters.

I said he would have to exercise it, "use it or lose it" is what I said, and I could see he liked the sound of that, the *oozes* and *its*, the affirmation. I told him to listen closely, to talk to himself, to say it out loud. I told him to read or write something every day, a poem, a paragraph, a letter, and be wary of distractions and diversions.

And every day it seems a game of chance. A clean page, another version, new griefs and meters, a fresh deck of possibilities. In Reno it is played as if there's no tomorrow. We look like robots, humanoids putting tokens in machines, waiting for the payoff, hoping for a sign, or killing time until our time kills us.

But we could all be alive tomorrow and if so we'll need some better answers than these games afford us. After a long night of winning or losing, it's good to have a desert close at hand into which one could do worse than to wander, like holy ones of old, to listen for the voices in the air or to raise up songs of thanks or to curse the luck or praise the name of whatever is out there listening, or isn't.

Afterword

*simply turn around and look
back. Like Orpheus, like Mrs. Lot, you
will be petrified—astonished—to learn
memory is endless, life very long,
and you—you are immortal after all.*

—RICHARD HOWARD

Time Time Time

n 1975, when my father was my age, he had a bronze plate engraved with his name and numbers on it. *Edward Lynch*, it read, *1924–1999*. He put it on a bronze casket in our casket showroom to demonstrate how the upmarket units could be customized. It was a sales aid. There's no telling whether it ever worked.

The nod to his mortality, full of Cagneyesque bravado, was instructive. Someday, he seemed to be saying at fifty, he'd be dead. He was right. The numbers are, after all, convincing on this, hovering as they do around 100 percent. What he also seemed to be saying was that he would only inhabit the twentieth century. He was right about that part too. He and my mother are both dead now, together forever in heaven and Holy Sepulchre, spared the worries over Y2K, end times, any more wars or rumors of wars.

Like millions of the moms and dads whose couplings begat the baby boom, my parents are forever fixed in the twentieth century whilst I and my siblings and my generation sally forth into the future. Sharp grief has grown into glad remembrance. They are gone but not forgotten.

Still, all through this dull season of saints and souls, leaf fall and blood sport, constricting days, and all through this gathering hoopla over the holidays and New Ages, there's been this odd little ache, just now articulated, that once the calendar turns we will be leaving behind, with once-every-millennium certainty, all those lovers and loved ones, memories and dreams that will become forever twentieth-century inhabitants, permanent fixtures of the old millennium and more distantly past tense. They will become "the former things" in a way that days or years or decades changing could not make them. Mean time, it turns out, has its gradations too. The list of things likewise consigned gets longer if we let it, thus: our childhoods, our children's childhoods, our grandparents and the "sixties" and that cheery illusion, easily maintained till now, that the future always outweighs the past.

Is this middle age or millennial angst?

"AND THEY ALL PRETEND THEY'RE ORPHANS," Tom Waits sings with stinging wisdom, "and their memory's like a train,/ you can see it getting smaller as it pulls away."

Does the last month of the last year of the last decade of the last century of the second millennium vex us more than most Decembers? Does the new broom of January 1, 2000, sweep cleaner than the one that swept 1950 into 1951?

For me it does, as it sweeps not only my first kiss in my first '56 Chevy Coupe but Henry Ford, the Industrial Revolution, free-market capitalism and the early formation of nation states into the apocalyptic bin. The same gulp of Greenwich Mean Time will swallow, in a moment and twinkling, the Beatles' *Revolver* album, the revolver that killed President Garfield. the French Revolution and the discovery of gunpowder. The shoe of history drops on the lot as we move from the decrepitude of one millennium into the infancy of another.

To have lived in two centuries is a fine thing. To be alive in two millennia is a much, much rarer thing. Genghis Khan didn't do it, nor Mohandas Gandhi, nor Mother Teresa, nor Edna St. Vincent Millay nor St. Paul. But Charles Manson will and Slobodan Milosevic and, please God, Seamus Heaney and Pavarotti and another six billion of our species-mates. The notion is laden with portent and omen. Waiting for time's advancing tidal wave we wonder what can be saved from the almost certain flood.

But if a New Age makes it harder to hold on to the best of our pasts, it makes it easier to let go of what was worst. Our fears, our distempers, our ancient feuds—each can be more easily assigned to old ways of thinking, old ways of doing things. The marriages that failed, the families we did not have, the hurtful, hateful words, the roads not taken can be left behind, like so much ballast and brouhaha. Regrets and good riddance are near enough twins.

"And it's time, time, time that you love," Waits croons in his chorus.

And why wouldn't we? For time bears its burden effortlessly—our loves and losses, hopes and remembrances, our parents and babies, good laughs and good cries. Time heals and holds us in its embrace. The future is a place we can travel lightly into, hopeful and afloat—all of our unfinished business finished by default—time runs out, runs on, with or without us.

Notes on
Frontispieces

For assistance with the selection and preparation of frontispieces the author is indebted to Patrick Young and Lori Mott of the University of Michigan Museum of Art, Ann Arbor, Michigan; to Len Grant for original photographs from his collection *A Way of Life*, published by Len Grant Photography, Manchester, England, 1999; and to Robin Robertson.

Page 29: "Cemetery Worker." Original photograph by Len Grant (British), 1999.

Page 37: "A. France & Son." Original photograph by Nico Sweeney, 1999.

Page 49: "The Little Nude Model Reading." Lithograph by James McNeill Whistler (American), 1890. University of Michigan Museum of Art. Bequest of Margaret Watson Parker.

Page 59: "Plate 61." Anatomical illustration by Andreas Vesalius (Belgian), 16th century.

Page 79: "The Musings of the Solitary Walker." Oil on canvas by René Magritte (Belgian), 1926. © 2000 C. Herscovici, Brussels/Artists Rights Society (ARS), New York.

Page 93: "Self-Portrait." Oil on canvas by Sean Lynch, 1998.

Page 115: "The Poet and the Muse." Lithograph by Henri Fantin-Latour (French), 1883. University of Michigan Museum of Art. Gift of Jean Paul Slusser.

Page 123: "'61 Pontiac." Lithograph by Robert Bechtle (American), 1968. University of Michigan Museum of Art.

Page 137: "Allegory of the Holy Catholic Faith." Pen and brown ink with gray wash and black chalk drawing by Marcantonio Franceschini (Italian), 17th century. University of Michigan Museum of Art. Gift through the Estate of Edward Sonnenschein.

Page 149: "Natural Habitat." Photograph by Tommy Lynch, from the author's collection.

Page 159: "What a Position." Lithograph by Paul Wunderlich (German), 1967. University of Michigan Museum of Art. Gift of Mr. and Mrs. Charles D. Clark.

Page 165: "Funeral Director." Original photograph by Len Grant (British), 1999.

Page 189: "Funeral Director." Original photograph by Len Grant (British), 1999.

Page 197: "The Fables: The Cat Metamorphosed into a Woman (11:18)." Drypoint and etching by Marc Chagall (French), 1928–31. © 2000 ADAGP, Artists Rights Society (ARS), New York.

Page 229: "Death Leading an Old Man to Grave." Etching and engraving. by Stefano della Bella (Italian), 1648.

Page 235: "Plate 22." Anatomical illustration by Andreas Vesalius (Belgian), 16th century.

Page 245: "Nora Lynch, 1970." Original photograph from the author's collection.

Page 251: "Scene in the Desert." Albumen print by J. Pascal Sabah (Turkish), 1880. The University of Michigan Museum of Art. Transfer from the Kelsey Museum of Archaeology.

About the Author

THOMAS LYNCH *is the author of three collections of poems. His book of essays,* The Undertaking, *won an American Book Award and was a finalist for the National Book Award. His work has been published widely in the United States, the United Kingdom and Ireland. He lives in Milford, Michigan, where he is the funeral director, and in West Clare, where he keeps an ancestral cottage.*